THE COLE PORTER STORY

By Richard G. Hubler

Fiction:

Non-fiction:

THE
COLE PORTER

THE WORLD PUBLISHING COMPANY

STORY

AS TOLD TO

RICHARD G. HUBLER

WITH AN INTRODUCTION BY

ARTHUR SCHWARTZ

CLEVELAND AND NEW YORK

Published by The World Publishing Company
2231 West 110th Street, Cleveland, Ohio 44102

Published simultaneously in Canada by Nelson, Foster & Scott Ltd.

Portions of this material originally appeared in The Los Angeles
Magazine copyright 1964, 1965.

Library of Congress Catalog Card Number: 65-23352

Printed in the United States of America.

HC-1265

The following photographs are from Culver Pictures—Cole Porter
at various early ages (3); Nelson Eddy and Ilona Massey; Nelson
Eddy and Eleanor Powell (2); Fred Astaire and Claire Luce;
Ginger Rogers and Fred Astaire (2); William Gaxton, Benay
Venuta, and Victor Moore; Ethel Merman; Ann Sothern; Cole
Porter and Moss Hart; Cole Porter at "Jubilee" rehearsal; Cole
Porter and Jack Kennedy; Jimmy Stewart, Buddy Ebsen, and
Eleanor Powell; Eleanor Powell; Bert Lahr and Ethel Merman;
Bert Lahr and Betty Grable; Fred Astaire and Eleanor Powell;
Bobby Clark; Danny Kaye; Cole Porter and Bella Spewack; Cole
Porter, Lisa Kirk, and Alfred Drake; Alfred Drake; Cole Porter
and Mike Todd; Cole Porter; Ginny Simms and Gary Grant; Cary
Grant and Monty Woolley. The following photographs are from
Brown Brothers—Cole Porter and showgirls; "Fifty Million
Frenchmen" (3); Fred Waring; Fred Astaire, Claire Luce, and
Erik Rhodes; Cole Porter, Clifton Webb, and Gilbert Miller;
Cole Porter after his accident.

To Jane

THE COLE PORTER STORY

INTRODUCTION

INTRODUCTION

IT WAS 1931 WHEN I first met Cole Porter. He was already a tremendous success, with six or seven Broadway shows behind him; and I had just written my first complete score—the music for *The Band Wagon*.

Cole called me up and introduced himself: "This is Cole Porter, your fan." He added that he heard I was planning a holiday in France, and if I liked, he would be happy to give me some letters of introduction to people in Paris and on the Riviera who might be interesting to meet. We made a date for the next afternoon at Cole's apartment. After a charming hour of tea and mutual admiration, Cole went to his desk and presented me with twelve hand-written letters.

I was overcome by his thoughtfulness and generosity, but when I made the trip I found I was unwilling to impose upon more than three of his friends.

It was a wise decision. Had I met all of them, I surely would have needed a holiday to recuperate from their hospitality.

In later years, I learned that Cole had extended himself to many other song writers whose work he admired.

He was one of the few geniuses of the theatre who could appreciate keenly the work of his contemporaries.

In response, I think that every talented writer of words or music who lived in his time agreed that no one wrote wittier or more beautiful songs than Cole.

I had a special opportunity to make this estimate when in 1944 I was a motion-picture producer at Warner Brothers. Jack Warner had purchased from Cole the rights to make a picture about his life, to be called *Night and Day*. Cary Grant was to play Cole, and I was assigned as producer. Naturally I studied every song he had written, and met with him frequently to discuss the ultimate choices for inclusion in the picture.

I learned from him (and from Dr. Albert Sirmay, his brilliant musical editor and amanuensis) how meticulous a worker Cole was. He could concentrate for hours at a time on a single phrase of music or lyrics. Sometimes he would work round the clock to finish a song. On one occasion, in Hollywood, he wrote seven different complete versions of the song "Rosalie" before he was satisfied.

He would verify factual or metaphorical allusions in his huge collection of reference books: thesauruses, rhyming dictionaries, encyclopaedias. He would tackle a song by seeking first a beginning phrase of words and melody, then the ending, and finally the material between the two.

This method of his explains the sharpness and cleverness of some of his marvelous endings:

"But if, baby, I'm the bottom,
    You're the top."

"It was great fun
But it was just one
Of those things."

"And this torment won't be through
Till you let me spend my life making love to you
Day and night,
Night and Day."

Musically (and financially) the film *Night and Day* was a great success, but the story suffered from insufficient dramatic incident and conflict. Apart from Cole's fabulous accomplishment, the only dramatic thing that ever happened to him was the horrible accident in which he was thrown from a horse while riding with friends. Both legs were crushed, and he underwent more than thirty operations to save them.

But even with this terrible affliction, Cole continued to write shows and picture scores of enormous vitality and beauty.

Where was the suspense in this plot? Where was the conflict? He was phenomenally gifted and very rich, he had an incredibly beautiful wife, his name was the proverbial household word, and celebrated people the world over sought his companionship.

He and I both knew that these were not quite the elements of great story-making. But we also knew that fictionalizing was out of the question. Audiences wanted to meet the real Cole Porter.

So we settled for the truth, which made for a rather predictable success story saved by glorious music. Cole and I weren't satisfied, but the public was.

While it may seem difficult to believe, the critics were not frequently kind to Cole's work. Except for *Anything Goes* and *Kiss Me, Kate*, most of his scores received luke-warm reviews. I recall that in 1935, when his show *Jubilee* opened, the press was chilly. Not a single critic mentioned the two great songs which emerged later as gigantic hits: "Begin the Beguine" and "Just One of Those Things." Similarly, in 1953, the songs from *Can-Can* were unappreciated in spite of the delightful "I Love Paris," "C'est Magnifique," and several other songs which have become standards.

Cole was debonair in his acceptance of the critics' non-acceptance. Opening nights, the bugaboos of most play-wrights and composers, were occasions of celebration for him. He invariably sat down front surrounded by friends, and laughed and applauded as if he were merely a spectator.

It was he who warned me early in my career not to expect good notices, but to await the public's judgment. "A joke can be told once and be appreciated," he said, "but a song must be heard repeatedly before it sinks in."

He has hardly been surpassed by any other writer in the number of songs that have "sunk in" and are played and sung by people all over the world.

That is his ultimate tribute. But there was a special one he treasured as much as any. It came in the form of an opening-night telegram from Irving Berlin some years ago. Paraphrasing one of his own famous songs, Irving wrote to Cole: "Anything I can do you can do better."

ARTHUR SCHWARTZ

THE COLE PORTER STORY

Cole Porter plays and sings his songs for the showgirls as a new musical begins rehear

ONE

FOR A FEW MONTHS in the summer of 1954, I was possibly the closest companion of Cole Albert Porter. Not because of any special social compatibility—though that seemed to exist—but because I was a writer and he was a subject who had offered himself for examination. He had expressed, through his public relations man (he had hired one, though God knows why he felt he needed publicity), his willingness to do a series of articles about his life. I was approached and asked if I would be willing to undertake the project. I considered it a compliment. But, at the same time, I felt that it would be worthwhile only if Porter read and checked the manuscript and agreed to allow his name to be used on it. This was agreed to.

We met at the side of his Romanesque pool at his house in Brentwood. It was as nearly his residence as any place might be, though he did not own it. For more than twenty years he had rented it from a well-known Hollywood designer. He had made it his own: it expressed perfectly his longing for isolation and peace. It was a place of deep cushions, muted colors, low half-lit rooms filled with the moving shadows of the trees outside. It was a place of silence, of wide polished floors, glints of metal, and pleasant odors—with his omnipresent grand piano, his lifelong chaperon, dark-shining in a corner.

This was the spot to which the composer came from such public accommodations as the Waldorf Towers in New York. At such times he wanted a retreat, a private cell of luxury, in which he could hide. Not for the sake of composing, for this went on endlessly, in or out of company. But in these years he hated to be with his friends when he could not be gay and he was in constant, increasing pain with his infected legs. My feeling was that I had been called in almost in the role of a consulting physician; it seemed to give Porter some ease to recall his life.

My impression was that Porter was a small man in repose. But I noticed when he was talking or playing the piano—not too well—he seemed almost perceptibly bigger. He literally gained stature from his work. When he chose, he could dominate a group with his personality but he did not often make that choice. He had a big-eyed, sensitive face—extraordinarily calm for a man who had suffered as much and as long as he had—with a well-tanned skin. What little remained of his hair was combed precisely in the middle. He spoke softly, without undue emphasis, but with an unusual clarity of recollection. I invariably checked out what he said and discussed his errors with him at our next meeting. He was not often wrong.

What he told me, during those long afternoon interviews, I took down faithfully. We did not meet every day because sometimes his legs (of which he never complained) gave him too much torture. On some occasions what I read back to him was not an exact reconstruction and he gently corrected me. What came out of it is, as far as I know, the only memoir that he left—a casual, sophisticated, almost cheerful look backward.

"What shall we call it?" he asked me suddenly, halfway through our talks.

His question caught me by surprise. I had just arrived that noon. The butler had turned off the enormous fan laden with insecticide which served to clear the area of gnats; lunch was on its way. Porter glanced at me and readjusted his faded bathrobe over his legs—he was always conscious of their presence, as if they were unwelcome parasites attached to his flesh.

"I don't know," I said. I hazarded: "Why not 'Don't Fence Me In'?"

"Why do you think that would be good?"

"It's the name of one of your songs," I said inanely. "And you've lived as you pleased, all around the world. You've had the money and the leisure to do what you wanted. Not many people can say that they haven't been fenced in by life."

A shadow crossed his face. He looked quickly down, then into the shimmering depths of the pool. He frowned.

"No," he said at last, "that's not quite right. It's a little too much. Besides, I never liked that song. It wasn't entirely original."

3

We left it at that. We never discussed it again. What his memoir was to be titled was never decided. But here, in virtually his own words (read, corrected, and approved by him) is what Cole Porter told me about himself in 1954.

TWO

MY GRANDFATHER, JAMES OMAR COLE, was a hearty man with a high temper who always considered me extravagant. He used to drive me a couple of miles out into the rolling Indiana countryside and rein in his horse at the top of a rise. He would point with the end of his buggywhip at a large, rather bleak gray building.

"That, Cole," he would say with satisfaction, "is the place where you will end up."

It was the county poorhouse. I was only eight in those days.

Getting home from such a gruesome sightseeing, I would rush to my mother Kate for comfort. She would hug me, saying indignantly: "Cole, don't listen to a thing he says! When your grandfather was a young gold miner in California, he had a personal valet!"

It appears to be the opinion of the general public that Cole Porter, the lucky fellow, was born with a twenty-

5

four-carat nugget in his mouth and a saleable song on his lips. When the motion picture *Night and Day*, based on my life, was made in 1946—a confection in nine reels that had no resemblance to reality but which has grossed more than $16,000,000 to date and is still doing well in some odd parts of the world—the script writers grumbled. Because, they said, "Porter has had no dramatic conflict in his life." Walter Winchell made a pithy comment on my wedding: "Boy with $1 million weds girl with $2 million."

I should like to attack this charming superstition, even if I cannot destroy it. It is true that after writing thirty-two complete musical comedy shows—twenty-six of them appearing in London and on Broadway, seventy-five percent of them being hits that gave a more than barely discernible return on the investment of what today would amount to more than $12,000,000—I feel that I may have succeeded.

After having written approximately fifteen hundred songs and lyrics, I am venerable enough at the well-preserved age of sixty-three (I was born in 1891, not in 1893 as my doting friends insist) to be called, together with my friend Irving Berlin, "one of the deans of American popular music." Let me add in a well-modulated voice that I have done the scores for eight movies and been handsomely rewarded for it. I have even composed a classical ballet, *Within the Quota*, which was performed in 1923 by the Swedish Ballet Company, in Europe and the United States, with great acclaim. Unhappily, the company is now defunct. The original music sheets are lost and I have no copies. My one effort to be respectable must remain in limbo.

He always dressed with considerable style and he was taught to ride at an early age.

In addition, I must confess that I inherited from my grandfather and my mother several millions that grew from his discovery of about $200,000 worth of gold in California in 1850—and his subsequent purchase of West Virginia timber-and-coal lands. I might as well add that these days my income from my songs puts me in the ninety-two-per-cent tax bracket.

But what few people know—and those who do, choose to blithely disregard it—is that for nine hard and miserable years, I was the most outstanding failure in the musical world. My productions were turned down every year as regularly as the tolling of a bell. One of the big four of the musical producers operating in those days, Charles Dillingham said: "Your words are amusing and I loathe your music." Florenz Ziegfeld declared: "Porter's attempts at music are either ridiculous or disgusting." Sam Harris informed me for more than a decade: "Nothing this year, Cole, but maybe next." For years Vinton Freedley was consistently kind while my hair turned gray: "We'll let you know, Cole, if we can use you." My friends told me in chorus: "Dear Cole, you're much too sophisticated for the general public. Your songs are all right to amuse us but you'll never make anything out of them. Think of your work as a hobby."

As for me, I went on grimly studying at such schools as the Schola Cantorum in Paris under the great composer M. Vincent d'Indy. I took composition, orchestration, counterpoint, and harmony year after year—and was resented by the French students for continuing to write in the abrupt, rhythmic American idiom. Berlin, effortlessly making his own niche in musical history in

8

New York, assured me: "Cole, you've got to live on Tin Pan Alley and learn to write like the rest of us."

My first musical was produced on Broadway in 1916. It was titled by a phrase that I invented and that has since become famous: *See America First.* I wrote the music. T. Lawrason Riggs, an old Harvard Law schoolmate, wrote the libretto and we collaborated on the lyrics.

It cost the equivalent of $250,000 and opened with fanfare. It closed within three weeks to the most unanimous chorus of derision ever heard in New York. One critic wrote: "I understand that the two authors are from out of town. I advise them to return to wherever they came from and stay there."

Riggs was so crushed by the universal ridicule that he never again wrote another word for musical comedy. Instead he became a convert to the Roman Catholic Church; shortly after he joined the priesthood and became, of all things, the chaplain at Yale. My own reaction was not quite as final but nearly so: within three months, I left for overseas and ultimately became a recruit in the French Foreign Legion after some desultory World War I relief work.

This disastrous outcome of my first venture into the world of professional musical comedy was a stunning setback to a career that all my family's friends had earmarked for triumph. My relatives did not view my leaning toward music so amiably: my grandfather despised it as the occupation of a nincompoop and my father Samuel, a scientific agriculturist, simply did not allow it to disturb him. It was my mother—a dark-haired, viva-

9

cious, very pretty woman—who kept my faith in my own talent alive. My second composition (the first was an obnoxious item called "Song of the Birds") was a burbling item called "The Bob-o-link Waltz." I wrote it at the age of ten. My mother was enthusiastic enough about it personally to carry the manuscript from Peru, Indiana, where we lived, to Chicago. She had it published. She paid $100 for a hundred copies. She distributed these at random among our friends. Even today, some well-meaning acquaintance will run across a yellowing specimen and send it to me as a gift.

My mother started me off on piano and violin at the age of six—twice a week, commuting thirty miles to the nearby town of Marion to take my lessons. I hated the violin with its squeaks and groans, chiefly because its case was so unwieldly; I gave it up surreptitiously ten years later at Worcester Academy in Massachusetts. I loved the piano from the beginning. For fifty years I have never lived in a house or apartment without a piano nearby. Even at prep school and college I had an upright in my room.

Even so, piano practise was tedious. If I became tired, my mother would take over and play burlesques of popular tunes such as "Ben Bolt." I remember laughing hardest at her rendition: "Oh, don't yew re-huh-mem-buh swuh-heet Al-liss, Ben Bo-holt," a satire next to sacrilege for those days. She was also responsible for making me theatre-crazy; each year we went to Chicago for two weeks of stage and opera. My introduction to the latter came when I blundered into the Auditorium Opera House backstage and saw a fat man roaring out a song at the top of his lungs, standing inside a huge white swan which was being hauled across the stage by a pair of concealed, sweating stagehands. That was my first encounter with Richard Wagner's *Lohengrin*. I was enchanted.

My own peculiar talents in musical composition first came to light at Worcester. I indulged in writing songs that today would be considered rather boring in any good café but then were damned as downright risqué. One was called "Fi Fi, Fifi," and another "The Bearded Lady." I sang them to assorted groups, including a select number of the faculty. Finally the headmaster called me in. After hearing one, he threatened me with expulsion if I wrote more. I continued writing, of course, and my friends said nothing about it.

I graduated from Worcester in 1909 as valedictorian of my class—largely because I had a sympathetic Greek teacher who suddenly opened the door to Homer and the New Testament in that language. For the first time I saw the music inherent in all words. Since then I have never been satisfied to write music and allow someone else to do the lyrics—I have realized that each must be wedded inseparably to the other. For achieving class valedictorian, my grandfather gave me a present of a grand tour of France, Switzerland, and Germany—implanting a love for Europe that I never lost.

Entering Yale as a member of the class of 1913, I merely stepped up my production of songs. During my four years there I must have composed more than three hundred. From my sophomore year onward, I did the scores for two shows annually—one for the Yale Smoker and the other for the Delta Kappa Epsilon fraternity. I also belonged to the Yale Glee and Mandolin clubs.

With them, I toured the country, playing at the piano and rendering my own compositions. I was considered a howling success by everyone, including myself.

One number that was my favorite, a burlesqued version of that lush ballad "Heaven Will Protect the Working Girl," was heard by the Yale dean. He called me in for a conference.

"Really, Cole," he said, "the way you sing that song makes for ill-feeling among the lower classes. I wish you would drop it from your repertoire." I made it my leading number.

I also entered the numerous competitions that Yale held every year for song writers. I got more than my share of prizes. My collegiate fame is still secure as the composer of "Bingo" (Bingo, bingo, that's the lingo!) and "Bulldog" (Bulldog! Bulldog! Bow wow wow! Eli Yale!), which are still sung lustily by the old grads at Yale football games.

Incidentally, both these songs were pirated by a little publisher in New Haven. They were put out by him with due credit to me, but I never got a cent of royalties. I also played a couple of songs during my college years for an emissary from the Shubert brothers—producers in New York. They used both tunes but never paid me.

These cultural and financial setbacks did not deter my ambition. I went on and entered the Harvard Law School to dig into torts and escheats. At one of the first smokers held by the school, I appeared onstage to do my stint and was heard—as usual—by the dean, a kindly gentleman named Thayer.

After I had left the stage amid the customary tumultuous applause, Thayer took me aside. I braced myself for the inevitable dressing down. To my surprise he did nothing of the sort.

"I want to tell you something that may injure your self-esteem," Thayer began, "but I think it is best for you. Frankly, Cole, your law marks are abominable. You will never be a lawyer. But your music is very good, indeed. I suggest that you switch over to the excellent music school we have here and say nothing about it to anyone. Thus they will be gaining a talented student and we will be losing a wretched one."

I did as Thayer suggested. I have never regretted it. Only my mother knew about my changing of majors. She told no one. It had been my grandfather's idea that I should be a lawyer and I had never liked it anyway.

I roomed with Riggs. We teamed up and gave impromptu performances of all the works for which we could find sight-reading recruits. It was our mutual enthusiasm for sophisticated social satire which projected us into the fiasco of *See America First*.

Despite this disaster—which involved such well-known friends of the arts as Elsie de Wolf (later Lady Mendl), Elizabeth Marbury, and Anne Morgan, one of the daughters of the famous financier J. P. Morgan—I did get to know two remarkable characters. One was a young Indianapolis ballet dancer of talent with a dry, sarcastic wit. His name was Clifton Webb; he performed very well, dressed in red leaves, in a number called "Autumn Dance." The other was a brilliant youngster just down from the hills of Dartmouth, who organized the production with professional éclat: his name was Walter Wanger.

After the musical closed, I lived in disgrace at the Yale

Club. I refused to see any of my friends. I left for Europe. There, after a time, I discovered I could join the Legion merely by being weighed. I signed up and was off as an *aspirant* (cadet) to the artillery school in Fontainebleau. Since I could speak French fairly well—I had spent a couple of summers with French families—I was finally ordered to liaison work with Americans. I was assigned near the front, close to Verdun, and billeted with officers who taught me French history and *chansons*.

In those far-off days an American in France was a freak of sorts. I was highly cherished as a mascot by the regiment. After some months, we were moved up for an attack near Nancy; we were told that this would break the back of the Germans but that few of us would get out alive. On the morning before the scheduled advance, the Armistice was announced. I shall never forget the exquisite feeling of relief with which I saw the pink-and-gold sunrise and the green French countryside. After all, I was a song writer, not a hero.

I went on to help out in the first occupation of Germany. I was regarded with wonder wherever I went. It was something I could not understand until a woman bolder than the rest, in a German village, stepped up to me.

"I always thought all Americans were black," she said shyly.

Finally I was attached to the American Embassy in Paris under Barclay Warburton. There I met my wife.

At that time, Linda Lee Thomas was considered not only the most beautiful woman in Paris but in the world —by those who knew her and certainly by me. When we met, it was one of those odd, inexplicable things that

Paris has always been—Paris. The girls were lovely, and William Gaxton, the guide, brought lots of laughs to Fifty Million Frenchmen.

make one believe it is possible that marriages are made in heaven. That we were created for each other I implicitly believe. It was Linda who supported my faith in my music through the long, dead years; who never gave up even when I did. Her merciful death in May, 1954, after a long siege of illness—even though I had expected it—was one of the most numbing blows I have ever felt.

We wanted to be married instantly but there were obstacles in the way. I was still a French soldier. My $500-a-month allowance had been cut to a fifth by my grandfather when he had heard about my abandoning law for music; and Linda herself was wealthy. I was determined to be able to support her. A banker-friend of mine, William Crocker of San Francisco, helped me; hearing of my grandfather's rage, he sent me $500 a month himself, telling me to accept it for as long as I needed it. (About nine years later, after I had ceased to need it, I sent him a check for more than $10,000.)

I had to have a regular income before I married, I felt. It was given to me providentially in the form of a return ticket on a steamer from Paris to New York. Aboard the ship I met the foremost American revue comedian, Raymond Hitchcock. I had been writing songs at various times and places during the war—ditties ranging from comedy ("Since I Got the Grippe Espanola") to love ("When I Had a Uniform On")—and had a selected collection of about two dozen. A friend persuaded Hitchcock to listen to me play and sing at the piano in the ship's main dining room, late one night. He sat rocklike and deadpan. Then, when I had discouragedly finished, he rose.

"I'll take every song for my new show, *Hitchy-Koo of 1919*," he told me.

In New York he introduced me to Max Dreyfus of the Chappell Music Company, who had discovered Jerome Kern, Vincent Youmans, and George Gershwin. Dreyfus has been my friend and publisher ever since. I finished the *Hitchy-Koo* score in New York and the show opened in Philadelphia. It was an instant smash and ran for two years. The oddest fact about it was that only one of my songs turned out to be a hit—and that by accident.

Shortly before the show opened, Ziegfeld had phoned Dillingham, Hitchcock's producer.

"I've got some old flower costumes I couldn't use in my Follies this year," he said. "You're welcome to them if you want them." Dillingham accepted; Hitchock came to me and asked for a tune to go with them. I sat down and, in a day, wrote "Old-Fashioned Garden." It was cut from the show and then put back to fill a stage wait. It became the hit of the production (together with the costumes). Within a few years I realized more than $100,000 from royalties.

"That song," I remarked jubilantly to a friend, "takes the place of my grandfather."

As a curious footnote, I may say that "Old-Fashioned Garden" was a dud in England, where most of my songs are hits. The odd reason, I discovered, was that the English are enthusiastic gardeners. I—in my botanical ignorance—had a variety of flowers blooming together that could never have appeared in each other's company.

The show was produced in the fall of 1919. Linda and I were married in December, in Paris, in the same year.

I thought my career was launched. I could not have been more wrong. I assailed the port of New York every year with a fresh score. From every producer I got flat turndowns as an "expatriate musician" or as a "too-serious and highbrow" composer. Each year I returned wretchedly to Europe to lick my wounds. To occupy my time, I kept scribbliing notes on bar-sheets—though I never wrote anything out in full—and traveling and learning. Linda and I discovered a unique summer resort, the Riviera in France, on the advice of Mary Garden, the opera star, and lived a gay life in Paris as well.

During those years, musically expatriate as I was, I managed with Linda to make our Paris house a come-all-ye for those who knew the passwords of art and music. Among our visitors was Anita Loos, a little girl with big eyes and bangs who had just written a naughty novel; Serge Diaghilev, a little, ruthless perfectionist whose creed was never to keep any dancer over thirty in his Russian ballet; F. Scott Fitzgerald, already an author of repute and a crying drunk and bore; Berlin, who had just offended New York high society by marrying Ellin Mackay, one of its brightest names. Berlin, a gentle soul, was so wounded by this snobbism that he found himself unable to write songs for a year—a loss of immense dimensions to popular music.

Miss Garden, the dynamic little Scottish opera star who spoke with a broad Middle-Western accent (as I did *not* by then), was there. Nellie Melba was one of our guests, with her cold perfect voice; so was Artur Rubinstein, a brilliant rising pianist, who played his best when primed on my vintage champagne; lean Igor Stravinsky, witty and sardonic in his terse French; Grace

Moore, and her greatest of friends, Vincent Youmans, the composer. Grace could never move very well on the stage, so Berlin wrote "All Alone by the Telephone" for her to sing in 1924: she could sit and sing enchantingly and never have to get about.

Others who came there were Pablo Picasso, the painter; George Gershwin, always with at least a dozen of his friends and relatives, playing all night his inexhaustible repertoire of his own compositions; and the then Prince of Wales, a terribly shy, amazingly blond young man who was in love—at the time—solely with American music. I recall that once, at the Duke of Alba's in Spain, hearing some of the most remarkable flamenco tunes in existence, he drew me out onto the balcony. "Cole," he whispered, "what wouldn't I give for just five minutes of good old American ragtime!"

Noel Coward, advancing relentlessly on his tide of genius and throwing off more quips in an evening than he did in a play, came to visit us. So did Moss Hart, viewing timidly the great and reluctant to talk about traveling because Paris and New York had constituted his whole grand tour; Fannie Brice, with her frank comments; impish Bea Lillie; the bouncing Douglas Fairbanks, Senior, with his sweetfaced wife, Mary Pickford—all these were among our guests in Paris.

But, even in the midst of the hubbub that was our home, I could not forget that I was as yet without fulfilment of my ambitions in music. I was overjoyed to get a cable from Hitchcock in the spring of 1921. He wanted me to write the score for his *Hitchy-Koo* of that year.

The show was produced by the Shuberts and due to open in Philadelphia. Linda sailed the Atlantic and arrived on opening night in the City of Brotherly Love just in time to meet my long face.

"All my songs are thrown out," I said tersely.

It was not quite true; two out of two dozen were kept, but they never amounted to anything.

Back we went to Europe—to France, Italy, Sicily, and Egypt. We hired a houseboat and went for a two-month cruise up the Nile. I was in charge. I hired nothing but musicians, actors, and dancers for the crew. Everywhere we stopped we had an impromptu show.

One of the guides we had in our amateur archaeology hikes in the Valley of the Kings was a tall, lean fellow named Mohamet Aboudi. He resembled an ascetic holy man and spent much of his time changing robes—of which he must have had more than fifty. Linda was so bewitched with him that I took him back to Paris with us as our butler. He spent two years in service and then, one day, came solemnly in.

"I've fallen in love with a girl who is a diver by profession," he said to me.

"You mean you want to give notice?" I inquired.

"Oh, no, Mr. Porter," he assured me. "I am going to marry her. I wonder if you would be good enough to put in a swimming pool so that she would feel at home." I fired him.

We visited in Spain with the Duke of Alba in his massive mansions in Seville and Granada that were built before Columbus discovered America, before Tin Pan Alley was even a dream. We attended opera not only in Milan but in every small Italian town—where the artists were often better than those at the highly touted La Scala. I did everything and anything, from Egyptology to mah-jongg, to forget composition, though I could not escape from my regime of daily study.

In 1923 my grandfather died, at the age of ninety-five. He left half his fortune to my mother. She promptly signed over half of her inheritance to me. It was a bonanza that gave me the chance to fulfil a childhood vow I had made to a theatre curtain in Peru, Indiana. As a boy I had been fascinated by that fantastic, painted view of the Grand Canal of Venice.

"Now," I said to Linda, "we'll have our *palazzo* and start our Venetian life, just as I said I would back in Peru."

It was not what I really wanted—what I wanted more than anything was success on Broadway—but it was a reasonable facsimile of something to do. Linda and I got up very early each morning to go sightseeing; I took painting lessons and copied old prints and did oils on glass. I soon discovered that my artistic talent in this field was less than negligible.

The same year of 1924 I met John Murray Anderson in Paris. He told me he was opening his *Greenwich Village Follies* and that he would hire me to write the score. I dashed for New York and completed the score. Linda sailed to see the opening in Philadelphia—and once more got there just as the producer tossed out everything I had done. Two songs survived that debacle: "Two Little Babes in the Wood" and "I'm in Love Again." I went back to Europe: to alternate fits of entertaining and despondency, studying music and history trying to get myself out of a black mood of despair.

The legends about the whole European idyll of Linda and myself are greatly exaggerated, I may say here. It is true that we bought a $250,000 house in Paris with zebra rugs and a platinum-leaf room, but we rarely used it. We were generally somewhere else—in England, Italy, or Spain. As for the four-year lease on the Palazzo Rezzonico, it is true we held parties which the social set of that day felt to be a little dazzling. The opinion as to which was the most vulgar was divided between the one where we had six hundred guests and fifty gondoliers for guard, with spotlighted tightrope walkers and fancy dress, and the one where Diaghilev brought his ballet company to dance and I supplied him with fireworks, a fifty-foot statue of Venus, and two hundred thousand candles to light up the sky. I personally was proudest of my *galleggiante*. This was a gigantic barge that held one hundred fifty guests. I designed it for a Venetian hotel and it plied the canals for months, loaded with visitors, with a French chef, a colored Dixieland band, a wine cellar, and a ten-dollar cover charge.

Four years of this and I met the producer E. Ray Goetz, on the beach at Lido. He had a new show with his wife, Irene Bordoni, coming up on Broadway. He tentatively suggested that I write the score. I fell on him like an over-eager puppy.

At any rate, I wrote the music and held my breath as Goetz approved of it—and actually kept it in the show. The production, called *Paris*, was an instant smash. I was a musical comedy writer in demand—and I was never again really in the doldrums after 1928.

It was not until a couple years later, however, that I was truly sure of my arrival in the musical world. The incident that convinced me came when I visited London and met the Lord Chamberlain. He greeted me with a smile.

"You know, Mr. Porter," he said, "I'm supposed to be the official censor on works like your musicals. I do wish to congratulate you on your scientific research in one song—I believe, 'Let's Do It—Let's Fall in Love.'"

"Scientific research?" I was a little taken aback.

"You know," said the Lord Chamberlain confidentially. He hummed a few bars. "'Birds do it, bees do it,' and so forth. That's quite scientifically accurate, my boy. 'Let's fall in love.'" The same song was later bowdlerized for fear of offending some of the minority races I had unwittingly mentioned in the lyrics.

In 1929 I was thirty-eight years old and expanding like a night-blooming flower. Goetz had another idea for a musical—the story of an American tourist in Paris. It was produced in the autumn, simultaneously with the stock market crash. It made no difference: the show, coyly called *Fifty Million Frenchmen*, was a smash hit. It contained my second standard, "You Do Something to Me." A standard, by the way, is a hit which goes on into all eternity of copyright and royalty; a song writer can tell when it happens when his publishers issue it in black and white without mentioning the show from which it came. I might mention here that I have never had a hit—as have most other song writers—apart from a musical show, though I have a library of some forty-three standards. It seems I need the stimulation provided by the integration of my musical ideas into a book and plot.

Fifty Million Frenchmen was notable for starting a cute vaudeville comedienne, Helen Broderick, on her

23

way and for the antics of William Gaxton. Norman Bel Geddes did his usual photographic sets for the show; Warner Brothers backed it to the equivalent of $300,000. It was the Brothers W. who were our downfall: they simply waited until they got their money back (in about six months) and then closed the show to make a repulsively bad picture out of it.

Wake Up and Dream, backed by Charles B. Cochran, the English producer, had also come out earlier in 1929. It had a song titled "What Is This Thing Called Love?" in line with my habit of using the word "thing" in my songs. Possibly I do it because it is such a wonderfully singable word. It was the first tune I had written where I shifted from a minor to a major key at pleasure. This slight experimentation in popular music frustrated the orchestras of the day so thoroughly that many bands refused to play it. They said that the odd beat confused their drummers. (I had picked it up in North Africa, in a square at Marrakesh where the dancers from the hills used to perform.)

This syncopation was a result of my first trip around the world, undertaken to get away from the doleful closing of *Fifty Million Frenchmen*. Linda and I sailed to the Far East where—I must confess—I found the music of India, China, Japan, Cambodia, and the other Eastern countries completely unintelligible. I was musician enough to follow it with my mind, but the soul of it escaped me. It was not until I went to Bali that I could hear the rhythms in my own head. I knew I had heard beauties in Oriental music; until Bali I could never tell *why* they were beautiful, to my own satisfaction.

Out of this trip, I believe, came all the foundation for

my enduring works. My two best songs, in my opinion, are "Begin the Beguine" and "Night and Day." They owe their conception to such Eastern music. Nevertheless I think I must also make a bow to the French, who taught me to use the extra phrase in music and to lighten my writing; to the English, who gave me relatively little except the warning never to speed up a tune for the sake of jazz. It was Africa that gave me basic beats, Bali that taught me the value of changing tempos and keys. Italy supplied the idea of pure melody, and Egypt the Oriental scale. It was Spain and its flamenco tunes which gave me —as they do to nearly every musician—the abiding influence of all these things at their purest and most primitive. In America, of course, I learned the native musical sureness of the Negro and the invaluable idea of direct, simple rhythm. These last were the greatest of all lessons to me: forcing me, as they had Gershwin, to abandon false sophistication for direct communication in music.

Places have always inspired my writing. I composed "You're the Top" floating along the German Rhine in a *faltboot* after a party where my guests had tried to make up superlatives to top each other; I did "Night and Day" on the beach at Newport. "Begin the Beguine" came from a war-dance chant I heard when we made port at a small island in the East Indies, but the title came from my having gone to a night club on the Left Bank in Paris where people from Martinique danced their local folk dance, an intricate bit called the *beguine*.

After *Fifty Million Frenchmen*, Linda and I took up residence in Paris and New York. We lived abroad six months, then came back to America to work for another six. It was wonderful living, commuting across the At-

"Rosalie" took much rewriting. Nelson Eddy and Eleanor Powell, Ilona Massey,

—and Miss Powell.

lantic, but my personal hex was catching up to me. In 1931 Goetz came to my flat with another show idea. I pounded out my usual twenty-song score in less than three months.

One evening shortly after the score was done, Goetz called on me. Wearing a sad smile, he said: "Cole, the show's out."

"Why?" I demanded.

"Cigarettes just had an extra tax put on them."

I was astounded but Goetz was right. He had a verbal agreement with a large cigarette company to put up the money. When the tax came in, our scared backing backed out.

Linda and I sped back to Europe for solace, spending Christmas in the *gemütlich* spirit aboard a German freighter.

In Paris, the rotund form of Gilbert Miller appeared with a Viennese comedy which he wanted to transform into a musical. He and I struggled with this work, called *The Spell*, for six months; then we christened it *The Smell* and gave up. Back in New York in 1932, Dwight Wyman told me a novel conception.

"Adele Astaire just got married," he said. "I want to star Fred Astaire alone."

Such a thing as one Astaire had never been heard of on Broadway. I agreed that it might be an excellent idea —though Fred was more than a trifle dubious about the whole business. The musical was called *The Gay Divorce* (Hollywood later renamed it *Gay Divorcée*, apparently on the theory that it sounded sexier). The play opened in Boston to very bad notices. Fred was as touchy as gunpowder at the opening. He complained that my songs had too much range for his voice and he indulged a collection of minor feuds backstage. He spent hours alone rehearsing and rehearsing—I have never seen a man work so hard. After a bare survival in Boston, the book was entirely rewritten. It opened in New York to the total animosity of the press, offended by "Cole Porter's brandied friends" who attended the first night in tails and decolleté. It came through after a dosage of cutrate tickets, but it was a near thing. It contained a tune no one noticed: "Night and Day," a tune Fred was at first reluctant to sing because of its wide range.

It took perhaps three months for that tune to get under way. It had forty-eight measures in the refrain instead of the usual thirty-two—a device I was the first to use in this country. None of the bands liked it at first. Suddenly it caught on. It flared up all over the world into the biggest hit I have ever had.

Perhaps I forgot to mention that there was another musical produced by Goetz sandwiched in somewhere during those hectic years. It was *The New Yorkers*. The cast was fabulous, including such stars as Hope Williams, Fred Waring's orchestra, and the greatest trio in show business, Clayton, Jackson, and Durante. The trouble was that, although the show was a huge smash, it cost so much in salaries and sets that Goetz lost money every second it was on the boards. It played for six months. There was no theatre in New York big enough to hold it and make Goetz a profit. He went broke. The consoling item about it for me was the fact that I managed to introduce a song I had concocted one night while strolling the streets of London. It was called "Love for Sale." It became one of my string of standard hits, but the lyrics and the subject banned it forever from the radio (and apparently the TV) networks as a song.

I had written the score for *The New Yorkers* directly after my tour that year of Mittel-Europa. Stuffing myself in the company of Ferenc Molnar and other famous playwrights in Budapest and Vienna, especially on a gourmet's delicacy, a rich cabbage pie, I had managed some good musical ideas.

But what I consider the best score I ever wrote—which was a flat popular failure—was the music that accompanied a London production for Cochran based on a novel called *Nymph Errant*. I did this in 1933. A Hollywood motion picture company bought it and, naturally, never produced it.

The most famous show with which I was associated was commenced in 1934. Vinton Freedley, who now admired my writing, had the idea of hiring P. G. Wodehouse, the English novelist of nonsense, and an associate, Guy Bolton, to do a libretto about a romance aboard ship. Writing from Le Touquet, one of the gambling centers of France, the Wodehouse-Bolton combine sent in a first draft so bad that it was obvious that the work was completely inadequate. Howard Lindsay, a new director-actor who later became famous as father in *Life with Father*—was putting on the show. I, through some of my friends, got hold of a newspaper reporter and publicity agent named Russell Crouse, who had an enviable reputation among the writers of New York. He and Lindsay undertook the rewrite. We had also hired a new girl singer, an ex-typist whose name was Ethel Zimmerman. She had changed it—in the interests of theatre marquees and billboards—to Ethel Merman. She had a voice like a trombone and a manner as ingratiating as a performance of a three-ring circus.

The script was finished and Victor Moore and Gaxton obliged by joining the cast—but just then the tragic disaster of the Morro Castle happened. We all agreed a ship comedy had no place on a stunned seaboard and rewrote the script once more. Gaxton, coming through the stage door one night, plaintively demanded of the doorkeeper: "What are we going to call this musical mishmosh?" The doorkeeper shrugged, grinned, and said: "Well, you know, Mr. Gaxton, anything goes."

The show was thereupon christened. *Anything Goes* was launched. Ethel, like Fred, was a little nervous about my wide-range songs. I had to give an audition for her mother, father, and agent. I rewrote "Blow, Gabriel, Blow," for her voice. She was right on that but I was right in sticking to my version of the others she was worried about: "You're the Top," "All Through the Night," "I Get a Kick out of You," and "Anything Goes." This show gave me five hit standards, the peak of my career.

Moss Hart, writer and psychoanalytic *bon vivant*, saw the show. He called me up for lunch the next day. Between drinks and finger bowls, he expounded an idea which it had given him for a show. He called it *Jubilee*. "But where can we find time and peace and quiet enough to write it?" I asked.

"We'll go to a foreign country," Moss said.

"Which one?"

"All of them!" he said. Three days later, we were booked for a round-the-world cruise.

We took six months to complete our trek. It was

wonderful—and we worked on the way sufficiently to have the complete score and book by the time we returned.

Mary Boland was the star. The show was a success until she decided she could no longer stay away from her swimming pool in Hollywood. She persuaded her agent to tell of a fictitious picture she was contracted to do and off she went. She was so popular that the show dropped off $10,000 the first week, $20,000 the next. We closed after a few weeks.

My consolation was that I myself had a legitimate contract to do a couple of scores for Metro-Goldwyn-Mayer, my first essay into pictures. I had completed my most famous song, "Begin the Beguine." This had appeared in *Jubilee* but its reception was chilly. It took much longer even than "Night and Day" to get going. It was five years before it was more than a failure and then, after such a long interval, it revived into popularity only when Artie Shaw did a swing arrangement. Another song, "Just One of Those Things," took even longer to emerge from *Jubilee* obscurity: ten years. "Why Shouldn't I?" also became a musical comedy classic.

The next ten years were those of my greatest productivity—hampered only by an accident which finally proved to be a spur rather than a hindrance. I was to become a close friend of Ethel Merman. I never ceased to be astonished at her habit of taking down lyrics in shorthand and of using her extraordinary voice in such a prodigal way. Arturo Toscanini said of her, in his classical maestro fashion: "She does not possess a voice but another instrument in the band." I know nothing

32

Fred Waring (The Pennsylvanians are not seen) in Porter's The New Yorkers, *1931.*

The Broadway musical success was called The Gay
Divorce. It had Fred Astaire, Claire Luce, Erik Rhodes
—and those wonderful, wonderful Cole Porter songs.

The Hollywood smash was called The Gay Divorcée. It had Fred Astaire, Ginger Rogers, Erik Rhodes, Edward Everett Horton—and those very same **Cole** Porter songs.

about that; only that whenever Ethel opens her mouth to sing it constitutes an event for me. I discovered she had a phenomenal idea of pitch and could even flat notes slightly, successfully, for comedy. It was she who accounted for the fact that *Anything Goes* was the first of my two "perfect" shows—musicals that had no tinkering whatever on them after opening night. (The other, *Kiss Me, Kate*, was a tribute to the assembled stagecraft of those associated with me.)

I learned to understand about Victor Moore, one of a series of sad comedians I knew who invariably worried about their parts. Moore complained bitterly that in one of his roles—that of ambassador to Russia with Sophie Tucker as his wife—he had not a single funny line. We pointed out that the audience was rolling in the aisles each night. He grunted suspiciously: "You must have your friends planted out there, you and the writer!" Fred Astaire became a good friend—a perfectionist who would not let the slightest note or step escape his voice or his feet without working them over and over and over.

Above all I gradually acquired an armor against the critics. In those days—and still today, though Rodgers and Hammerstein have managed to educate them to some extent—no tune that a musically illiterate critic could not whistle as he went up the aisle at the end of the show was a good tune. Perhaps I am more sensitive to this foible of the gentlemen in the free seats than most— inasmuch as my songs do not seem to be whistleable until some time after the show. I had been a success first in Europe, with the Latin quality I had learned to put into my music, but America became at last even more generous with applause and appreciation. It was Linda who, above all before my Broadway success, kept me working and experimenting in spite of the critics and producers who could not see whatever virtues there were in my music.

It is a curious fact, however, that once I was established I seemed to be an old hand to the cynics. Linda and I, seeing review after review of my shows containing the phrase: "Cole Porter was not up to his usual standard," burrowed back to the very beginning of our file of clippings. We discovered, not very much to our surprise, that there was no such thing as my "usual standard." The critics had forgotten to set one in the first place and had merely commenced using the phrase.

In 1936 Freedley asked me for a show to star Durante and Merman. That was the genesis of *Red, Hot, and Blue*. This show, with such performers, could not help being a hit from the beginning. The only hitch came when it was discovered that both Merman and Durante had contract clauses that called for their names to be listed first. This presented an insoluble difficulty until I cut the Gordian knot. I suggested that the names be presented by being printed in the form of an X—Durante going down and Merman up. Even this did not entirely meet with their agents' approval. Every two weeks the names were changed, Durante going up and Merman reading down. I became thoroughly acquainted with Durante during the run of a year. I can say only that he is one of the few saints of the theatre—his kindliness is exceeded only by his talents.

Two of my songs intrigued me in this show. The first, "It's Delightful, It's Delicious, It's Delovely," was inspired by a chance remark of a friend. Coming into Rio harbor during one of our tours, Linda and I saw the sunrise. "It's delightful," she murmured. "It's delicious," I said, feeling the cool air. Monty Woolley, staggering out of the depths of sleep behind us, said loudly: "It's delovely!" The song was born. The second tune was one that has never been popular but I have always been fond of it—it is so exactly suited to the personality it was written for. Freedley wanted a special song for Merman. I wrote "Down in the Depths on the 90th Floor." It was a smash the opening night; the second night it was a flop. It has continued so ever since—but I still have a fondness for it.

The next year I was riding in Long Island one early morning. I took my horse up a mildly steep hill. It was wet and slippery. My horse shied at some bushes—I did not pull back on the reins, as some insisted afterward—and he reared and fell on me. I woke up in a local hospital with both legs broken in compound fractures, an important nerve nearly cut in two.

From then on, I spent months under sedatives. Through the years, I underwent thirty-three bone operations under the jurisdiction of John J. Moorhead, the best bone surgeon we could find. For nearly a decade it was a moot question whether or not both legs would have to be amputated below the knee. Luckily, it proved that this was not needed; and though today I still walk with a decided limp, I go under my own power and on my own flesh and bone.

That first year of intense pain, I did two complete shows. This was under the express orders of Dr. Moorhead.

"Work!" he said emphatically. "Work as you've never worked before!"

I believed him. I think it saved my mind as well as my legs. I have always loved writing music and lyrics as nothing else in my life. My semi-doped brain seemed to be buzzing with tunes. To keep at my writing, I had my piano raised on wooden blocks and sat at it in a wheelchair. My habit of working out words and tune in my head before experimenting with it on the keyboard helped as well. I wrote *You Never Know*, with Clifton Webb, who had appeared in my first fiasco in 1916, as the star. There was a mutual bond between us that nothing could sever, a cord welded by that original failure and my present misery. The show was produced by the Shubert brothers. It was a success in a small intimate theatre in Philadelphia; put into the huge Winter Garden in New York, it was an immense flop.

The second show was called *Leave It to Me*. It starred Moore and Sophie Tucker again. June Knight, a charming singer, had one of the most prominent numbers of the score, a tune called "My Heart Belongs to Daddy." We felt that she—being in love herself with a Texas millionaire at the time—could give it the requisite punch. Suddenly she married the man and retired from the stage. We were *vis-à-vis* auditions.

An agent called me and said he had a client who might fit the role. I asked him up and he appeared, leading a dreary little girl who appeared to be the last word in scared dowdiness. My pianist played and she sang. I confess that such a moment is marked with five stars in my head: it was the finest audition I have ever heard.

"Dress her up!" I cried.

A star was born named Mary Martin. From that time forward, she sailed full steam ahead. Her voice and charm have been national assets ever since.

In the fall of 1939, Buddy de Sylva—himself a song writer and producer of motion pictures—dreamed up a show with Herbert Fields called *Du Barry Was a Lady*. It starred Bert Lahr and Merman, Lahr being next on my list of sad comics who keep alive the role of Pagliacci— clowns on stage, worriers off. De Sylva called me and said he was scared of the show without a moment of low sentiment in it; I said I would write a song for it. With my tongue in my cheek, I composed a ditty called "Friendship." It was one of the hits of the musical, as sung between Merman and Lahr. It was nonsense and the public loved it.

In 1940 and 1941, there were *Panama Hattie* and *Let's Face It*. In the former, I took a tip from de Sylva's instinct for sentiment and agreed with him that a composition to diddle the public into tears would be useful at the box office. I wrote a tune called "Let's Be Buddies." Sung by Merman to a rather annoying brat, it was hogwash but it made the box office dizzy for a year. *Let's Face It* starred Danny Kaye for the first time—a wonderful comedian with so much talent that he makes most of the others seem stupid. He was always on stage even with his friends, always happiest when he was wandering in public among his forest of dialects. I do not believe there is a language or patois on earth that Danny cannot imitate to perfection—and even, on occasion, improve with doubletalk.

The dress rehearsal of *Let's Face It* was the worst I have ever seen—so bad, indeed, that I called up all my

e players: William Gaxton, Benay Venuta, and Victor Moore. The show: Anything Goe

Ethel Merman knew how to sing Cole Porter's songs, just as he knew how to write them for her. Here she is on stage in Panama Hattie. *When the movie was made (below), Ann Sothern played the part of Hattie.*

friends and begged them not to come to opening night. Contrariwise, the opening was the most polished and winning of any of my shows (with my hit called "Everything I Love"). Kaye has since gone on to even greater heights but he still retains all his original, wonderful naiveté. I often think of him with terror as an innocent lost in the maze of his own virtuosity.

Something for the Boys and *Mexican Hayride* came in 1942 and 1943. My stream of hits was commencing to run a little thin, though the public still came to see them. Freedley, in the midst of producing the first, got cold feet. He announced he could not go on with the show, though we had a fine first act finished and were well into the second.

I had heard of a young and rising impresario who had just produced some Gilbert and Sullivan in swingtime, called *The Hot Mikado*. I phoned Mike Todd.

"I don't know you and you don't know me," I said. "That makes it a standoff. I'm writing a show with some friends of mine. Vinton Freedley has just refused to produce it. Will you step in? If you'd like, we could arrange an audition."

"I don't need to hear or see anything," said Mike. "If you're doing the music, I'll produce it."

It was a nice gesture on his part and the show was a nice success.

Mexican Hayride I never liked—but it was memorable to me for a bet I made with Woolley.

"The great Porter talent can never make a go of something banal," he said. "You must have something different in order to write a hit."

"Not necessarily," I said.

"Why don't you just write a song called 'I Love You'?" challenged Woolley.

I bet him five dollars I could. I set about it. I had a hard time getting it into the show and nearly lost the love of everyone connected with it. It was true the song had no real place in the score—but I felt I had to prove Woolley wrong. As it came out, I did; he paid me the fiver with bad grace, as the tune became one of my biggest hits.

The resentment among some of the show people was great enough, however, to start the rumor that Cole Porter was finished in the musical world—a prediction premature by some ten or twenty years, I should say. It was bolstered when, in 1944, I wrote the music for Billy Rose's *Seven Lively Arts*. That was a show which had Moss Hart and George Kaufman, Bea Lillie, and Bert Lahr, and should have been a success. Bea and I had some squabbles over her music and Billy Rose proved to be the wrong kind of impresario for a sophisticated musical. Perhaps my tunes were wrong, though I of course find it hard to admit it. At any rate, the show never got off the ground. It was a rank turkey.

At about this time, I commenced to think that the rumors of Broadway about my being through may have had some substance. I went traveling once more, with Linda bolstering my ego—always a rather frail and delicate bloom—until I felt I could write again. "Don't pay any attention to anyone except your own feelings about what is right in music," she assured me. I believed her where I believed no one else.

I was pleasantly surprised myself, in view of the supposed unsingability of my tunes, to hear that in 1948 five of my songs were among the thirty-five all-time favorites in this country—a record matched only by Berlin and not touched by any other composer.

During this time, I was engaging in the only other form of creative work I have ever undertaken (if the single early ballet is excepted): that is, scores for Hollywood motion pictures.

My introduction to that fabulous land was bizarre in the extreme. I spent my first Christmas there in 1936 while I was working on tunes for a picture called *Born to Dance*, which introduced Jimmy Stewart—who in turn introduced the song of widest range I ever wrote called "Easy to Love." Virginia Bruce sang "I've Got You Under My Skin" in the same picture, another which became a standard in the music library of the public.

It was not Stewart's personality nor his range of voice which impressed me as much as the Hollywood Christmas party I attended. This was held on the hottest, most sunshiny day I can recall—but everything was determinedly Christmasy, Vermont-style. There was a quartet, dressed in mackinaws, boots, and earmuffs, singing carols and sweating as if they had been in a Turkish bath; we drank hot Tom-and-Jerries; and the climax came when a thunderstorm roared up and soaked the southern California fir trees outside, making their tufts of absorbent cotton snow rather pathetic.

My producer on this picture, though he was paying me $3,000 a week and I was champing to work, insisted on sending me off to the desert to rest—so I had to sit in the desert from December to March, before I could begin to write four songs.

Rosalie, my next picture, in 1937, contained the title

song that became such a hit. I wrote six versions of this and none pleased MGM's Louis B. Mayer. He advised me: "Forget the six songs, Cole. Just write a honkytonk number." I did it and it turned out to be the hit, thus justifying his judgment. (I have saved the other six but only one now appeals to me.) This picture also had the melody, "In the Still of the Night."

I recall the *Broadway Melody of 1940* only because I was amazed to see Eleanor Powell dancing to my music and kicking $100,000 worth of gigantic drums at the same time. *You'll Never Get Rich*, at Columbia, should be remembered if only because Harry Cohn, the president of that company, insisted on having my score passed on by his secretary and telephone girls. It was a bad score but the girls said it was passable. It was a worse picture. Twentieth Century-Fox's picture *Something to Shout About* was something for me to cry about. I wrote only one hit in it "You'd Be So Nice to Come Home To."

Incidentally, my most famous "Western" song, "Don't Fence Me In," was a tune written for Twentieth Century-Fox in 1934. I bought the lyrics for $200 as a poem from an antediluvian cowhand. I wrote the tune with my cheek stuffed with tongue. I put in every Western cliché that I could think of and that my friends could suggest. It was never used by Fox. It made its way over to Warner Brothers and was used by them in a 1944 film called *Stage Door Canteen*. To my amazement, it was a gigantic hit.

When the *frères* Warner produced *Night and Day*, they wanted my songs—so they made the picture to fit them. If there is one thing my songs have never fitted,

*bove: Clifton Webb is flanked by Cole Porter and Gilbert Miller. Below: Moss Hart is
the enviable position of listening to Cole Porter as the songwriter goes to work on
e piano.*

Jubilee *goes into rehearsal in 1935 with Porter giving notes to stage manager (above)—watching action (below).*

it is my life. But they got the tunes and I got $300,000. It was an autobiographical mishmosh that demanded that Linda and I be separated because of plot—a flat lie, since we never had a harsh word of any kind. I asked for Cary Grant, the best-looking actor I could think of, to play the part of me. Cary was willing, but Warner Brothers was producing the picture and Cary was under contract to Columbia.

I persuaded Jack Warner to call Cohn. Cohn demanded, as the price of releasing Cary, that Jack have early morning breakfast with him. Jack refused flatly. It was only after weeks of my pleading that he abated his fury and had breakfast with Cohn—who promptly used it as the opening sentence in his conversations about Hollywood for the next few months: "This morning Jack Warner came over early and got me up to have breakfast . . . ."

This picture was also the bane of Woolley, who happened to be a star in it. He complained about too many Y's being on sweaters in the portrayal of Yale men. I backed him up. Woolley had been my close friend ever since our campus days and had traveled all over the world with me. We had cemented our friendship when he was a senior and I a sophomore by illegally bilking his father, a hotel-chain owner, of numerous bills. Woolley would smuggle us up to an unoccupied suite. We would have an orgy on the house—until his father caught wind of it and would telephone: "Monty, are any of those *things* up there?" a phrase indicating collegians. "If there are, throw them out!" Thus I felt Woolley to be an authority on anything resembling collegiate hijinks.

My next stage musical was in 1946, an affair which might have been a success—should have been, perhaps—except for the fluctuating backers. *Eighty Days Around the World* was set up, produced, and directed (and occasionally acted) by Orson Welles.

I have rarely admired a man so much. Welles did everything possible toward the success of the affair, going for one full week without food or sleep, subsisting on coffee. I was present when he called up one of the mighty in Hollywood and sold him a story plot over the phone for $25,000 to raise the money for the costumes—and then promptly forgot what he had sold. This fact later became part of the legend attributed to other writers, but it was Welles who actually did it.

The failure of this was so colossal that my own reputation suffered. It was not improved by my work on *The Pirate*, a $5,000,000 Hollywood picture that was unspeakably wretched, the worst that money could buy. I felt I was out of work; that no one wanted me. "Spread the word that I'm set to do another show," I told my agent. He shook his head. "Right now no one wants you, Cole," he said. "They think you're old-fashioned."

I commenced sweating on an idea with a soap-opera writer—if a notion of how desperate I was may be given—when the famous writing team of Sam and Bella Spewack came to me with the suggestion of doing Shakespeare's *Taming of the Shrew* as a musical. I swore it could not be done, whereupon they wrote a single scene. I read it, liked it, and wrote a single song. So the second great "perfect" hit was born. Oddly enough, the song I wrote, "We Shall Never Be Younger," was thrown out of the score because it was "too sad—it made everyone cry," according to the producers.

After rehabilitating my reputation by the success of *Kiss Me, Kate*—one of my two shows that never had any tinkering done to it after opening night—I took on the score of *Out of This World*. It was a failure. I was pleased with my own doings, but the book was bad, I thought. The scenery was so spectacularly great that the audiences looked at it and neither heard nor saw the actors. However, I got three standards from it—"Use Your Imagination," "Nobody's Chasing Me," and "I Am Loved." Then I supervised the Hollywood version of *Kiss Me, Kate*, and added to it a song dropped from *Out of This World* called "From This Moment On." It has since become a standard.

Up to the present, my last musical hit was *Can-Can* in 1953. This was based on Paris in 1893 and was, naturally, preceded with great research on the spot. Messrs. Feuer and Martin, the young producers, hired me because they felt I knew the locale—and they liked my music. I was delighted to work with them because of their thoroughness—they supervised every possible detail of the show. I think it was Feuer who corrected the buttonholes from 1894 back to 1893. At this writing, the show is still going full blast.

All of which brings me up to the present with the usual two questions anyone must face at my age.

What is ahead? Work, more work, I hope. People say I am ruthless about being bored; that my whole life is devoted to escaping boredom. Nothing could be more wrong. If working hard at my profession with social interludes is escaping boredom, then my friends have made the most of my foible.

What have I got out of life? Happiness, for the most part, and an income which has pleased me.

People have called me bitter-sweet, gay, off-color, complicated, and eccentric. I believe that my work is simply matching mood and color to the texture of plot. If anything, I am a self-adopted Latin and my songs are derived from the sultry, disillusioned South.

I am happiest when working alone on a new score with pad and pencil and rhyming dictionary. Next to that, I like to work with young people, the only continual challenge in our world. Dancers better than any, possibly, because they are the most joyous. They have no thought of the future; they are always healthy, without fear or care.

More than anything else, I enjoy a challenge. I am now writing another show, a musical based on the kidding of the Russian commissars. It is taken from the Ernest Lubitsch picture, *Ninotchka*. It is called *Silk Stockings*. I am doing my version of Russian melodies for the first time and I believe they are good—though I am not sure the show will be a success in view of the present state of international relations. One famous dance director refused to work on it: "Our situation with Russia is not something to make fun of."

I disagree. When we cannot laugh at our enemies, we are in a wretched position.

After giving most of the credit to myself for my success, with second billing to Linda, I should not forget Kate, my mother. From the time of the first success of *Hitchy-Koo* in 1919 in Chicago, she attended my hits or my misses. Fourth row center, those were her seats. And Kate always worried, as I do today, "what about the *next* show?" She died in 1952, at the age of ninety.

I still remember one remark of hers which I think was rather good. She was sitting next to Dr. Moorhead, the bone surgeon who had become one of my close friends, at the opening of *Kiss Me, Kate* in 1948. After the first half the curtain came down to tumultuous applause. Dr. Moorhead turned, smiling, to her.

"Well," he said, "Cole has another smash on his hands."

Kate shook her head. "I don't know," she said. "Let's wait and see the second act."

Which is the way I myself feel about my career. It's been a good first act. I'd like to see the second.

THREE

So far Cole Porter concerning himself. What he wished to present was a portrait of himself as he believed himself to be at the time, to the closing of what he felt was his "first act." The tone of our interviews had been frank and refreshing. They were concluded with regret on both sides.

But it was to be really near the end of the "second act." It was the last major interview of his life. Certainly he never permitted any further investigations of his life in this depth and scope—much less the use of his name—for the remaining decade of his life. Porter wanted the story of his career to end on a high note. He chose the 1948 *Kiss Me, Kate* premiere incident as a suitable climax, which also managed to include a graceful tribute to his mother—the real influence in his life.

In refusing to talk much about *Out of This World*, Porter stood on the fundamental rights of a craftsman who is disappointed when his skill does not produce the

54

desired results. He felt that its record of 157 performances represented comparative failure; moreover, he was
satisfied with his music and lyrics but felt that the show
as a whole was not up to par. As for *Can-Can*, it was still
glittering on the New York stage as we talked. Porter
was highly pleased with its opulence and pace (it lasted
892 nights). He was equally delighted with the popularity of the score—which had been a hit from the beginning—especially with "I Love Paris," which he
claimed had been inspired by the beautiful skyline set
built by Jo Mielziner for the show. The song later became the unofficial theme song of the real city, played
by hurdy-gurdies and sung by native *chanteuses*—despite
the fact that it was written by a farm-born American.

But Porter, in his heart, never even compared these
productions with what he considered his best score-and-
lyric job in *Kiss Me, Kate*. He considered that its run of
1,077 performances was just tribute to the indirect collaboration of himself and his associates with Shakespeare
(descended from *A Thousand and One Nights* through
Italian literature to a popular Elizabethan poem written
in a peculiarly Porterish vein, *A Merry Geste of a Shrewd
and Curst Wife in Lapped Morrelles Skin*). "Somebody
said that it was the perfect musical comedy," he told
me, "and I agree with them." As usual he was perfectly
frank about his musical virtues and his judgment was
objective and impeccable. He spent about a thousand
dollars to take nearly a hundred guests to see its opening
night. He himself returned time after time to view it
with complete artistic equanimity.

Still, despite his affection for *Kiss Me, Kate*, it was
Anything Goes which really held his heart. Here, Porter

felt, his music and words had been the major factor in making the show a hit (420 performances), in giving it coherence and pace, and in taking it over the jumps of what had been originally, in his opinion, a botched book. It was the love of a creator at the height of his powers who has a crippled brain-child and by sheer force of will makes it an admirable offspring. It was the spirit of his mother Kate all over again.

When we had finished the long word study of his life —and the homemade tomato juice of which he was inordinately proud—I went home, prepared the final manuscript, and delivered it. He took it and studied it, making a few corrections. He expressed himself as happy with what we had done and asked if he might hold his copy a few days to show it to some friends "for correction and amplification." I agreed without hesitation, since the whole enterprise depended upon his assent.

Less than a week later, Porter told me that he did not feel that the work could be published. "Not in my lifetime, anyway," he said, with his slight wry conversational smile that balanced his grin and booming laughter of real amusement. "I've been a little too frank about other people and even about myself, I suppose. If you don't mind, I'd rather it didn't appear while I'm still around."

After some argument about the labor and time expended—during which he offered to reimburse me and I refused—the only possible decision was reached. "I'm sorry I let you down," he said, in parting, "but after all you still have the manuscript." That was the last time we saw each other. I pleaded for reconsideration by wire —he had by then left for the East—but his reply was firm.

, *Hollywood!* Born to Dance. *Jimmy Stewart,*

Buddy Ebsen, and Eleanor Powell are all here.

Bert Lahr had one of his very best roles in Du Barry Was a Lady. He also was able to work with two very different leading ladies. On the left, we see him with Ethel Merman. Over on the right, Du Barry is played by Betty Grable.

For the next ten years I kept my word. The only tangible evidence of our collaboration that I received beyond the script was a gift from Porter. It was a book, a collection of the criticisms of Max Beerbohm in the London of 1898-1910. Porter's note, enclosing "a present," added that "you may like some of these." Whether it was pleasantry or afterthought, compliment or criticism, I never discovered.

Still to come was his words-and-music—then virtually completed—for *Silk Stockings* in 1955, a spoof on the Russians and Hollywood, where love was a "chemical reaction," but which ran for 478 appearances. Yet beyond this meagre—by his standards—triumph, nothing was ahead except some exquisite agony. He suffered from chronic osteomyelitis in his legs—the wonders of the antibiotic drugs had not been available in 1937. He underwent twenty-one operations on his legs in the ten years between 1938 and 1948 alone, thirty-three in all. He endured in silence until April, 1958, when his pain and general physical debilitation reached such an extent that he had to have his right leg amputated. He was sixty-seven at the time, but he learned to walk all over again on an artificial leg with the aid of canes—often relapsing, however, into a wheelchair.

Porter wrote nothing more, at least as far as Broadway shows were concerned. He noodled over his pianos but nothing of song-worthiness was announced. Dozens of hopeful musical comedy books, with or without backing, were submitted to him, and numerous movie scripts as well, but Porter skimmed them listlessly. His inspiration had gone. He felt no return of his will to compose: his unique concentration had been shattered by his bodily pain. When asked tactfully about his work, he replied: "I haven't gotten around to it." He had ended nearly sixty years of productiveness.

Nevertheless he kept up his usual yearly routine of living in New York from October to June, in a Waldorf Towers apartment with nine rooms and five bathrooms. It was filled with carefully chosen and grouped *objets d'art* which he and his wife had collected in various parts of the world, chiefly Paris. Every Friday noon, he took off behind his chauffeur and drove to Williamstown, Massachusetts. There he stayed in a cottage, surrounded by the records of his original musical scores and a tranquilizing view of the Berkshire Mountains. He and Linda had enjoyed rare peaceful moments here but, after her death, Porter had ordered the big house and its memories of gay parties torn down. He kept the cottage (which had formerly been his study) only because of sentiment.

Thus he spent his solitary weekends. His weekdays in New York were sometimes occupied in informal entertaining in his apartment—since he despised his crippled state and very rarely issued from his lair in the Towers. The dinners were elegant, replete with good food and bright conversation, timed and served perfectly—but Porter found that he tired easily. "I wilt before my boutonniere," he said regretfully to a friend.

He did not care any longer to see many people or to see them often. He became more and more of a recluse, not even going to the most exclusive theatrical affairs. But he never looked more than fifty, even in his seventies, and ten years dropped from that when he laughed. His conversation remained perceptive and witty, his appearance immaculate. But it may be guessed that before the end he grew tired of both his years and his talent.

Porter kept up his transcontinental commuting almost to the last, spending from June to October in Brentwood, California, on a quiet off-street in a society suburb. He had arrived early in September, 1964, to enter a hospital in nearby Santa Monica, to prepare for an operation to remove a kidney stone. The operation was successful but Porter had seemingly given up his joy in living. His physical condition had degenerated; his will to survive was wanting. On October 15, at about eleven o'clock in the evening—approximately the time when one of his Broadway shows would be rising to its climax—Cole Porter died.

The only attendants at his bedside were his two valets and his publicity man. They said he was "conscious but not lucid" when the end came and that he had died as he had always wanted to die—"suddenly, just like that." In his will Porter stipulated that he be cremated and that no funeral services be held. Most of his estate, in royalties amounting to an estimated $100,000 a year, went to a second cousin as his closest surviving relative. The administration of his effects was given to The Cole Porter Musical and Literary Trust.

Porter's possessions were scattered to institutions and individuals, as ruthlessly as his dust. In his own words, his life was "past all endeavor," unless something of his spirit remained in his musical heritage.

FOUR

IN ROUNDING OUT THE PICTURE of himself that Cole Porter offered to those interested, it should be said that biography is one of the uncertain sciences. Trapping the personality in print is a most dangerous game. All that ultimately appears in words seems to resolve itself into mere descriptions of actions, people, times, and places. The real characteristics of the subject always evade the right word, except in those few instances where there is a miraculous chance wedding.

There are three general types of such composition. All are unreliable. The traditional biography, written *post persona*, has the opportunity of perspective and relative freedom but it cannot be anything but impersonal. The impress of the living person is lost. And by simple destruction and selection of documents before death, the dead control the hand of the biographer to a great degree. Autobiography is even less dependable. The element of human vanity (as in the classic cases of Rousseau and Casanova, who intended complete frankness) obtrudes itself. The subject has a vision of himself in his head. He attempts to sketch it on paper and the result is most often a caricature.

The anxious author is left with what might be called the process of auto-amanuensis. This is the device of a person himself telling his story to an expert, bolstered by documents and cross-references, checked out by skillful cross-examination, explored by questions that attempt honestly to bring to the surface revealing facts, anecdotes, and examples. Though this "as told to" method is currently looked down upon, it may very well become the most effective and truthful portrayal possible. This, simply because it allows the writer of integrity to bring independent judgment to bear upon a living witness—who is the man in the dock and the jury at the same time, yet not the judge. It allows the individual to take advantage of his own impressions and the authority of his experiences—and who can speak more truly or feelingly than the man who has lived it? Beyond this, it permits the use of a large degree of objective inquiry and dispassionate standards of value.

At least this last method is that which Cole Porter selected. He knew it would be a flawed mirror, darkening in places, but then it is doubtful if he believed that any reflection of himself, however skillfully done, would be a fair resemblance. For his image to posterity, he appears to have trusted largely to the incommunicable nuances of his music allied to his lyrics.

A man remains most unknown to himself. His friends know him a little better; his enemies know him about as well as he can be known. To have no enemies is one of the tragedies of the world. Porter was a victim in this respect. He had many friends and acquaintances, but no one hated him. He had a wide range of habitat and was at home everywhere.

Those critics who tried to find him in the maze of his career have slid off his highly polished surfaces, catching at the boutonniere in his lapel or the gold garters on his leg to save themselves. Porter was possibly one of the most shy and retiring men alive. He retreated behind his façade of work whenever the world ceased to amuse him or, better, when it began to frighten him. Significantly enough, his three closest friends during his lifetime were three that he made during his undergraduate days at Yale University.

Porter needed protection but he did not ask understanding. He was aloof but he was moved to participate. He despised society but moved within it with an agility which has seldom been surpassed. Money and sophistication—each dependent on the other—were his trademarks but he coined ten times as much by his own efforts as he inherited. It is not altogether wrong to describe him as the country boy who became the compleat city slicker.

If examined candidly, his life is not at all complicated. Porter led one of the most simple and direct existences in the world. It was a way of whim against a background of inexorable duty toward his work. It is true that his path was simplified by plenty of funds and his joyous curiosity (one finds eyes as frank and questing as his only in the strange koala bear), but, in the end, it was his own continuing passion for the ways of his work which kept his inquisitive instincts active to the last.

65

Most of himself remains in his music—that remarkable duality between words and tunes that fit as tightly as though the opposite poles of a magnet brought them together. His words are tricky, involved, and tortured, sometimes pedantic, often cheap and suggestive. But although he was no wizard with language, he knew the essentials of the business he served and expressed it perfectly. On the other hand, his music was always adequate, often exquisite, and sometimes superbly classic. The chances are that Porter will be rated highly by posterity for his exploits in this area of his talents.

In both words and music Porter remained an experimentalist but in different degrees. He did not know enough or trust himself enough with vocabulary to approach innovation; he was a master of the catch phrase and the ordinary innuendo alone, not everlasting verse—and he confessed it. The contrast between his words and his music at this point is immense. Porter stretched the whole fabric of popular American music, squeezed it dry of sentiment, wrung it out in exotic composition until it became a whole new genre which foreshadowed what might be called "society-folk opera."

At the same time he had a contempt, perhaps a fear, of anything but amusement. He was not a message man. He did not have the faintest desire to contribute musically or verbally to either the woes or the lucubrations of the world. He simply wanted to sing in his own key (and he sang badly in person) to his own notes and ditties. He wanted to be unified for better or worse within the schizophrenia of his profession (unlike Gilbert and Sullivan, who hated each other at the last but found their partnership essential). Often his music and words seem

staire and Eleanor Powell do one of those lovely dances in the Broadway Melody.

Comics: Bobby Clark in Mexican Hayride; *Danny Kaye in* Let's Face It.

like a warring dialogue, arguing between themselves over which shall make the final impact upon the audience, and the music is always victor.

Porter was forever aware of his audience. He wanted desperately to please people—not necessarily as individuals but in the mass. Not because of any insecurity in himself but an insecurity that he felt about the whole absurdity which was the pattern of the world. If the world and man and woman were gossamer, as he feared they might be—and as many profound philosophers before him have guessed—then he would be a gorgeously jeweled spinner of tunes, throwing them out to ensnare as many as he could. Music was the way to his peculiar power. But in spite of the fact that he had this strength, that he was a kindly and courageous man, he was always a lonely man who wanted to lose himself in a crowd of glittering notes.

Porter could cast a cold eye upon himself. He refused to be caught in his own web. About his method of composition, for example, he declared that "my sole inspiration is a telephone call from a producer. If (he) phoned me today and asked me to write a new song for a spot, I'd just begin thinking. First, I'd think of an idea and then I'd fit it to a title. Then I'd go to work at the piano, spotting the title at certain moments in the melody and then write the lyric—the end, first—that way, it has a strong finish. It's important for a song to have a strong finish.

"I do the lyrics like I'd do a crossword puzzle. I try to give myself a metre which will make the lyrics as easy as possible to write without being banal. On top of the metre, I try to pick for my rhyme words of which there is a long list with the same ending.

"I'm becoming less and less interested in tricky rhymes. I think I used to go overboard on them. In Yale, I was rhyme-crazy. That was due to the fact that I was Gilbert and Sullivan crazy. They had a big influence on my life. My songs are easier than they used to be, musically and lyrically. I've never been able to get complete simplicity the way Berlin does. Sometimes I'll take twenty-five minutes to write a song, sometimes two days. I can tell a bad line by watching audiences. The minute they look at a program, I know the line has to be thrown out. Pretty often, though, you have to have a bad line so the next one'll look good."

Such an objective viewpoint about one's self says much for the honesty of Porter's thoughts about himself. He never minimized the work his compositions cost him any more than he would have deprecated a friend. They cost him most of his life and he was willing that this should be so because the rewards were what he wanted. "I've been accused of being remote," he said, "but that's not so. I've been working. I've done lots of work at dinner, sitting between two bores. I can feign listening beautifully and work. That's the reason I like to go out. I have no hours. I can work anywhere. I work very well when I'm shaving or when I'm in a taxi. When this horse fell on me, I was too stunned to be conscious of great pain, but until help came I worked on the lyrics for the songs for *You Never Know*, a song called 'At Long Last' in particular."

This habit of work, founded on an extraordinary gift of concentration, was with him from the beginning. His own estimate of songs—three times what is normally granted him in the records—is based upon what he actually did, not what appeared on the stage. His first were written when he was nine; the date of the last of his writings is impossible to guess. (Tunes like his "Bridget," for example, written in 1910, are not within the purview of the critic.)

It is apropos to consider Porter's surprising claim to have written fifteen hundred songs. It is far from unlikely. Three hundred of them he claims for his college days. Dividing the twelve hundred remaining among forty years—from 1913 to 1954—it would seem reasonable enough when it is remembered that Porter himself declared that he rarely took much more than two days to complete a song—sometimes less than half an hour. The conclusion is further bolstered by the fact that Porter's executors found a hundred more songs in his apartment after his death—and that Porter was counting up a grand total of all his compositions, whether he considered them worthy or not. Of these the public, of course, knows less than a hundred; the connoisseurs, about five hundred. The total of song copyrights by Porter, including some alternate arrangements, is 393. The hundred discovered in his apartment included such items as "Bertie and Gertie," "Dainty Quainty Me," "Dizzy Baby," "He Certainly Kills the Women," "Hip Hip Horray for Andy Jackson," "I Can Do Without Tea in My Teapot," "Just Another Page in Your Diary," "Why Do You Want to Hurt Me So?," "Wild Wedding Bells," and "My Louisa." These were sent, with the rest of the original Porter manuscripts, to the Yale collection as his will had requested.

It is interesting to conjecture about the influences which must have affected his song writing as a boy. Whatever his own opinion about his non-aloofness, certainly no exterior events in his childhood had much influence on his composing, precocious as it was. The last years of the nineteenth-century were crammed with wars —the Sino-Japanese war of 1894, the Italo-Abyssinian war of 1896, the Greco-Turkish war of 1897, the Spanish-American war of 1898, the Boer war of 1899, the Boxer insurrection of 1900, the Russo-Japanese war of 1904. But none of these left the faintest trace in his works. There were disasters galore, of the first magnitude—from President McKinley's assassination in 1901 to the eruption of Mount Pelee, with a loss of 30,000 lives, the next year and the San Francisco earthquake and fire in 1906— but Porter's childhood seems to contradict the psychological truism of youthful trauma in developing talent. His music and lyrics reflect none of the upheavals of those years. There is almost no martial beat in his works (as compared to, say, *Strike Up the Band*) and no beat at all of doom and gloom. As a matter of fact, his work remains very much the same from the beginning. There are generic similarities between "I've a Shooting Box in Scotland" (from the fifteen-performance *See America First* in 1916) and "Fated to Be Mated" in *Silk Stockings*. Porter's standard folio of songs goes all the way back to 1919 with "Old-Fashioned Garden" from the *Hitchy-Koo* of that year.

From the beginning, Porter's gift of withdrawal—so much noted by his friends and admitted by himself—was devoted to making his own world. One memory of his boyhood did stand out in his mind: the elephants in the

Wabash River that ran past his hometown of Peru, Indana. After the St. Louis World's Fair of 1904, the German zoo and exhibitor Hagenbeck, from Hamburg, Germany, organized a wild animal show. It developed into the Hagenbeck-Wallace Circus, and Peru gradually became its headquarters. Porter always admired the galumphing and trumpeting of the pachyderms taking their baths as much as he did the circus band. In 1943 he memorialized Indiana (which in 1938 had given him a testimonial letter and a bronze medal of which he was inordinately proud) in a patter song called "By the Mississinewah," attributed to a stream that flowed through his father's property.

The greatest single influence in his life and career came from his mother, Kate. She drove him to violin and piano with the lightest of whips, persuasion and humor. Porter hated the first for its "whiney" tone and because he had to carry it; he loved the second for its rich chords and the fact that someone else carried it. Even from the beginning, he was not inclined to physical effort unless it was wholly for the effort's sake. It was also Kate who, with her impromptu piano performances, introduced the element of satirization into his life; it became the steel spine of his songs. It was she who often took him the couple hundred miles from northern Indiana to Chicago and led him willingly and wide-eyed into the wonderful world of theatre and opera in Chicago. It is even possible that he saw some of the touring "musical comedies" of those days such as *The Merry Widow, Mlle. Modiste,* and *Floradora.*

"I've had two great women in my life," Porter said. "My mother, who thought I had this talent, and my wife, who kept goading me along, in spite of the general feeling that I couldn't appeal to the public."

Elements of these early impressions in sounds may be detected, one supposes, in Porter's music. But he escapes classification by the very force of his own dexterous gaiety and the occasional emotional sweep of such songs as "Begin the Beguine." He admitted to being a solemn "monkey-faced" child who thought the world was very serious and mysterious, not many years after he was born June 9, 1891, in Peru. He never forgot that 750-acre orchard farm of his father's—erroneously termed an "estate" by some commentators—and vowed that he would some day settle down there. He always claimed that he had been a farm boy in the real sense—hoeing, making hay, and the rest of it. "That's where I first learned to ride horses," he said.

Neither was he born rich, as some declared. The money came eventually from West Virginia, where his grandfather invested in coal and timberlands and made more than $7,000,000—Porter never liked to talk about the exact amount. The young grandson was promised a sixth of the inheritance on condition that he be a lawyer but this was later relaxed. The money fell to his share on his grandfather's death in 1923, just before he began writing the score for the *Greenwich Village Follies of 1924*.

Long before he knew what they meant, Porter fell in love with assonance and onomatopoeia, with synecdoche and syncopation. He was tuning words together before he lost his lisp. He dated his earliest song back to 1900 and a childish operetta called *Song of the Birds*, composed when he was ten. His "Bobolink Waltz" supposedly scandalized his grandfather but Porter continued his sly composing until he was packed off to Worcester Academy, Worcester, Massachusetts, to begin the process of sanding off his rough Mid-West spots. He graduated in due time at the top and was entered in Yale, emerging as a member of the class of 1913. These gay days were spent largely with wealthy socialite acquaintances such as William C. Bullitt, Monty Woolley (later one of his closest friends), Leonard Hanna, and Vanderbilt Webb.

His years of composing for college shows and improvising for his friends—a habit he never lost—gave Porter an impetus into the commercial aspect of popular composition. His friendships with the well-to-do and socially acceptable offered him cash backing. Thus, three years after graduation, he put on his first show with Riggs. How far out of line the Porter-Riggs affair was at the time can be gauged by pointing out that the great success the year before his graduation had been *Sumurun*, a lush, exotic German import in nine erotic and spectacular tableaux. In 1913 the competition was *The Passing Show* and the *Ziegfeld Follies* of that year, all sumptuous revues. Undoubtedly Porter and his Harvard lyricist had viewed the offerings of their rivals. What made them think that a callow all-American native production would succeed must remain a mystery. But their show went on and off almost as quickly as a light switch. It crushed both of them. They vanished from the Broadway scene. Porter holed up in the Yale Club, refusing to appear in public for weeks; as he said, "I thought I was a social pariah." He had lost his friends' money and his own self-respect, so inflated in his senior Yale year. When he looked back at it, he could afford to be lighthearted: "The reason for the flop was that no Yale man should ever try to write tunes to Harvard lyrics." But at the time it was an almost annihilating blow. Porter's shyness and basic inhibitions returned in full force. He went to France. He took a course with the French artillery school at Fontainebleau and even served as an American instructor at the front.

But he had not abandoned his music. He managed to take his own piano into the combat zone. It was a portable affair—"part zither, part harpsichord"—that he could strap to his back. On this he composed for whoever would listen and gradually his spirits returned. They were helped, according to rumor, by his meeting a beautiful canteen socialite, Mrs. Linda Lee Thomas, a fashionable Southern belle abroad to do her bit. She was the daughter of William P. Lee, a Louisville, Kentucky, banker, and had been married previously to E. R. Thomas, formerly publisher of the New York *Morning Telegraph*. It seemed up to Porter to match her fortune and up to her to wait for his tryst with fame.

Linda Thomas was the second and the last woman whom Porter loved. Not only because she was sophisticated and worldly-wise, lovely and charming—but also because he had played and sung for her after his fashion and she had believed in his potential. At the time he badly needed all the encouragement he could get. Not only the question mark of his talent but money was his problem. After he graduated from school with an ordinary degree and refused to go to law school more than a year, his grandfather had cut off his allowance of $500 a month. A banker friend replaced it and Porter much later repaid it. "My first recollection of that," Porter told me, "was that he tore up the check and sent the bits back to me. On second thought, he didn't; he cashed it. But what a nice gesture it would have been on his part." It was, it may be added, a gesture that Porter himself would probably have committed. (After 1928 and for thirty years thereafter, his income from composing alone averaged out at "well over $100,000" a year.)

The encounter with Hitchcock and the *Hitchy-Koo of 1919* was Porter's first leg upward in self-esteem (he received $12,000 for the two-year run). He returned to Paris, married his dream, and enrolled in the French schools to learn about the innards of music. He could not wedge himself into the Broadway cliques but society was easier. He and his wife set about a tour of Europe, unhampered by any other inhibitions than his dogged desire to succeed in popular music. He did not realize that his ambition was closer than ever. The true musical comedy form was slowly being hammered into shape by productions like *Bombo*, with Al Jolson; *The Perfect Fool* and *The Grab Bag*, with Ed Wynn—including songs like "He Eats French Dressing Every Night So He Can Wake up Oily in the Morning"—and a variety of unclassifiable *Frolics, Scandals, Follies, Whirls,* and *Revues.*

In Porter's later estimation, his success was delayed much too long. "There seemed to be a feeling that since I was not encamped in Times Square," he said ironically, "that I was out of touch and didn't belong. Once in a while I'd get jobs to do but some of them failed before reaching Broadway and I (his score, that is) was thrown out. So I traveled and discovered the world and kept on writing because that's what I most enjoyed. I had to wait some nine years before things began to click." What

77

particular efforts he made to become part of the American musical scene he refused to discuss, leaving only hints of his desperate days.

Nevertheless, his near-decade abroad was far from wasted. The Porter menage became the most sought-after, both in Europe and the United States. It was an international life that sometimes skimmed over as many as seven parties from dusk to dawn. The pair maintained plush lodgings in New York, Paris, Venice, and on the Lido. In Venice, they hired the Palazzo Rezzonico, where the poet Robert Browning had died, and they spent $4,000 a month to keep it up. Their Paris town house on the Rue Monsieur ("such an amusing name") had walls of mirrors and furniture upholstered in zebra skin, a fad later taken up by an American night-club. His hideaway in the Waldorf Towers had two apartments, one for reveling and the other for working. There were also "retreats" in Massachusetts and a modern home in Brentwood. The Porter parties were probably the most famous in the world at that time, especially those staged in Venice.

Despite his continual rejections by the major producers of Broadway shows, Porter carried quires of bar-sheets with him in his luggage and sturdily kept composing song after song. His sole success (as far as the public knew) at first was "I've Got a Shooting Box in Scotland," which had caught on from his *See America First* production in 1916. His next was "When I Had a Uniform On," "My Cosy Little Corner in the Ritz," and, most of all, "In an Old-Fashioned Garden" from 1919, a result of *Hitchy-Koo*'s fifty-six performances. The

Follies five years later was to be a comparative smash with 127 performances and songs such as "I'm in Love Again" and "Two Little Babes in the Wood." Starting in 1924, Porter's wife gave him a cigarette case for each opening. A sample case was the one she gave him for the opening of *Red, Hot, and Blue*. It was a platinum affair decorated with rubies (red), diamonds (hot), and sapphires (blue).

Porter disliked even implied criticism of his high living. He once cabled the family lawyer from Europe: PLEASE SEND ME $1000. REGARDS, COLE. The lawyer sent the check by mail and enclosed an austere note: "Cables cost money. In the future I will assume that I have your regards." To which Porter gaily cabled back: REGARDS, REGARDS, REGARDS, COLE.

Nevertheless, another hiatus of four years intervened before he got the job of partially doing *Paris*. There were other composers and lyricists involved with the Porter contributions. But his songs like "Let's Do It" far overshadowed the others. The next year, with *Fifty Million Frenchmen*, he was launched with a bottle of champagne, fairly on his own. After that, he shared his lyrics and tunes with no one.

Every year or two afterward for twenty years on, Broadway saw a new Porter musical comedy—sometimes two at a time. Porter helped out handsomely with his work in *Wake Up and Dream*, which opened just about a month after *Fifty Million Frenchmen;* he got the same help from others with *You Never Know* in 1938 (his own *Leave It to Me!* opened only three weeks afterward the same autumn). But these were the only two musical comedies where Porter allowed others to share the spot-light in the flood of some twenty productions that came after *Paris*.

His own style and renditions dominated the New York theatre which had so long rejected him. His travels paid off in intricate tourist lyrics which—in "You're the Top!"—rhymed Pisa with Mona Lisa. While sixteen-bar verses and thirty-two-bar choruses were the sacred cows of song writing, Porter amiably doubled the ante in both cases. He was not afraid of the repetitive note—"tick, tick, tock" and "beat-beat-beat"—nor was he daunted by the length and depth of a song. Some of his compositions ran over a hundred bars and stretched the tonsils of more than one singer—causing most of his arguments backstage with such performers as Merman and Astaire. He did not mind if his stars were not acceptable singers; his private opinion of the voices of the latter pair was rather low. What Porter wanted was "delivery" of the tune and, most especially, of the words in such a way as to get maximum audience impact. He thought no one sang "Night and Day" as well as Astaire, for example.

He was also careful to make his lyrics succulent for the singer. He wrote them only after studying the idiosyncrasies of his stars. He tried to include the word "terrific" in Merman songs because "she hit it like a sledge-hammer." For Bert Lahr's inimitable patois, he included such lines as "Now for ninstance, Snooks," in imitation of his spraying style of song. Mary Martin got lyrics as meltingly spiced as her personality in "My Heart Belongs to Daddy." As Porter remarked, "my inspiration, whatever that may be, doesn't come out of the thin air. It comes from people and places."

His words were not always felicitous. In one of his unpublished songs for *Anything Goes*—in accordance with his practise of coming up with several candidates— was the discarded "Waltz Down the Aisle." Its refrain ran:

For our bridesmaids we'll choose
Only dancers from revues
And only ushers who can turn somersaults;
And the old wedding march,
So pretentious and arch,
Will give way to a lively waltz.

His love for satire and impromptu entertaining some- times supplied him with additional ideas. Listening to a hillbilly program over the radio at a party, he suddenly sat down to improvise a burlesque of the songs and lyrics. But he got carried away in another direction with a satirical society dirge, "Miss Otis Regrets." It never won popularity in the United States but it caused enough hilarity in translation to sell more than a hundred thou- sand copies in Scandinavia and Hungary. It also served as an admirable comedy song for his friend Woolley, who bawled it out with emphasis on "leerics" at every possible society appearance. Possibly it was a social protest.

Elsa Maxwell, the society duenna and good friend of Porter, once related—in her own peculiar prose—how another tune of his was created on the spot. Said she: "Though Cole and I were both passionate playboy and playgirl, infusing new life, transfusing new blood into that thing erroneously known as 'society,' Cole secretly

Cole Porter and the Spewacks (Bella below) went to Shakespeare for Kiss Me, Kate. Alfred Drake and Lisa Kirk were the two leads.

despised it as much as I did. I will never forget one night when I had at least a dozen kings, or near kings, coming to dinner with me at the same time. It was my birthday, and Cole said: 'I have a present for you.'

"After the soup I was too impatient to wait longer and demanded 'Where is my present?' He got up, ran to the piano in the corner of the Ritz (Paris, of course) dining room, and this is what he sang:

I met a little friend of mine a week or two ago,
And he was all togged out.
I said "Forgive me, but I'd really like to know
What this is all about.
You're over-dressed—you're absurd."
He answered, "Don't say a word . . .

"I'm dining with Elsa, with Elsa supreme,
I'm going to meet Princesses
All in Coco Chanel dresses
Going wild over strawberries and cream.
I've got bromo seltzer to take when dinner ends,
For I'm dining with Elsa and her 99 MOST intimate
  friends."

Last night I met that little friend of mine once more
Dressed like a bold Apache.
I hardly knew him, for across his face he wore
A very false mustache.
I said, "But why this disguise?"
He whispered, "Don't put them wise . . .

"I'm dining with Maxwell, with Maxwell, my dear,
She's tired of Princesses
In their Coco Chanel dresses,
And she's longing for sausages and beer.
I've covered our tracks well,
For I'm saving Miss Maxwell
From her 99 MOST intimate friends."

On the other hand, Moss Hart recorded Porter's method of working in another mode. During their world trip—in the course of which they collaborated on *Jubilee* —he witnessed the birth of two songs out of the native scenery and customs. As Hart described it:

"At our first stop in Kingston, Jamaica, another side of his nature I had not bargained for was exhaustingly revealed. He was an indefatigable sight-seer, a tourist to end all tourists. No ruin was too small to be seen, particularly if it meant a long climb up a steep hill; no ride into the interior was too far, if it was a broiling hot day and there was a piddling waterfall at the end of it.

"The flora and fauna fascinated him, and he would drive miles to gape at a native shrub or an animal that flourished only in a particularly disagreeable part of the country. This insatiable tourism, it turned out, was also grist to his mill, which ground on whether he was sight-seeing, eating, or—for all I knew—sleeping. I made this discovery a few days later when I went to his cabin to hear the first song written for 'Jubilee.' It was called 'The Kling-Kling Bird on the Divi-Divi Tree.' I had heard him asking innumerable questions about this bird and tree during our Jamaica stopover.

"It did not surprise me too greatly when later on,

after we had left Samoa, he informed me that one of the chief ballads for the show was to be 'Begin the Beguine.' The Beguine was a native dance we had driven endless hot miles to witness. I had reservations about the length of the song. Indeed I am somewhat ashamed to record that I thought it had ended when he was only halfway through playing it. But I was much relieved that our chief love song was not to be about a koala bear or a duckbilled platypus which he had found entrancing."

Porter's own report on the composition of the song which many rate next to "Begin the Beguine" for immortality—the "Night and Day" he wrote for *The Gay Divorce*—is much more matter-of-fact. According to him, he wrote it merely to fill up a hole in the show—and almost as soon as it was heard, sociologists began talking about its weighty hidden meanings. This annoyed Porter.

"I wasn't trying to plumb any depths or interpret mass psychology of the times. Something new technically, though, crept into the number, willy nilly. I wrote it in forty-eight bars, against the sixteen bars traditional in popular songs up to 1932, and I widened the voice range to four notes over an octave. Both innovations handicapped the song in the beginning.

"I was living down at the Ritz-Carlton when the song was put together. I put the tune on paper, I remember, on a Saturday and wrote the lyric the next day while lying on a beach in Newport.

"Monty Woolley, the actor, had dropped in at the Ritz while I was at the piano Saturday night. 'I don't know what this is you are trying to do,' he said, 'but whatever it is throw it away; it's terrible.' However, I tried it out on some guests at a house party and they liked it."

Many of the stories about Porter's special sense of humor concern his pranks against society. At one point, hirsute-faced Woolley gave a formal New York party. Porter showed up with an unusual guest on his arm—the bearded lady from the circus. Woolley remonstrated with him loudly, in no uncertain terms. Porter heard him out until he had to take a breath, then coldly addressed his consort: "Madam, your son has atrocious manners."

An ancient colored woman who worked in the ladies' room of a night-club in Paris met Porter one night and confided to him that her greatest ambition was to spend an evening in the company of high society. Porter asked her which phase of that fictitious institution represented her dream. She replied that she dreamed of the famous Charity Ball which annually collected all the most famous names.

"Very well," Porter said, "I'll take you there."

"But, Mr. Porter, I don't have a dress for anything like that!" expostulated the amazed woman.

"I'll fix that, too," Porter advised her.

He got in touch with Molyneux, the dress designer, and ordered a duplicate of the gown that the most hoity-toity grand dame would be wearing. He presented it solemnly to his friend and duly escorted her to the ball. Whether it can be classed as a grand prank, a cruel hoax, or a sympathetic gesture is conjecturable.

In the thirties, Porter and Elsa Maxwell had a fake feud whereby he issued notices in her name of gorgeous parties, including the best-known names of the day—and, always, someone known as Mr. and Mrs. S. R. Fitch of Muskogee, Oklahoma. She and Porter kept the gag going for the summer (in imitation of the fiction that Evelyn Waugh had concocted the year previous). In the papers, they showed them about Europe in the company of royalty, cruising them on the Mediterranean with ancient titles and *nouveau riche*. Finally Miss Maxwell pulled the cork on the whole scheme. She announced that, though the fictitious Fitches were Porter house guests, they had stalked out to attend a party at Maxwell's. LAY OFF FITCHES IF YOU KNOW WHAT'S GOOD FOR YOU, Porter wired her. Miss Maxwell forthwith published a photograph of the unapproachable millionaire—a friend of hers in false whiskers and an old-fashioned bathing suit. "The Fitches are intolerable snobs," said Porter in his most dignified manner and let the matter drop.

Producers, who had a hard time locating Porter after his first successes, used trans-Atlantic cables to hunt him down. One received an answer that the composer was *faltbooting* down the Rhine. "That guy," muttered the producer. "Why can't he do his hiking at home?"

Porter's accident with a horse in the autumn of 1937—while riding at the Long Island Piping Rock Club in Locust Valley, with some titled friends—was the real turning point of his life. Porter was proud of his riding, next to his composing. He rarely grew angry but he reacted bitterly when the rumor went around that it was his fault. His equestrian critics insisted he must have pulled back on the reins of the horse that fell and crushed his legs—giving him the affliction which eventually killed him. He told me he always resented it: "I must tell you that I did nothing of the kind but I don't wish to blame it entirely on the horse. The ground was very slippery and perhaps I should not have urged him up the incline." Actually, his limbs were so mangled that the bones pierced the flesh; there was talk of amputation from the first but Porter fought it off for twenty years before he gave in. Typically, with a grim gayness, he called his left leg "Josephine" and his right leg "Geraldine." When finally the latter had to be taken off, he sighed: "Geraldine has been unfaithful to me, in her fashion." It was this terrible winter that inhibited his production of tunes for the musical *You Never Know* in 1938. But it was also during this agony of pain and suspense that he began organizing and composing words and music for *Leave It to Me*—almost between operations.

He drove himself now with an intensity unequalled before. *Du Barry Was a Lady* opened in December, 1939; it needed a little schmaltz, Porter felt, so he wrote a dripping ditty called "Friendship" to build sentiment. *You Never Know* had lasted only 78 performances, but this ran for 408. *Panama Hattie* came in October, 1940, and ran for 501 performances; *Let's Face It* (October, 1941) ran for 547.

For relaxation, Porter took to the radio. He became an addict of soap opera. In 1955 he told a reporter that his "sacred hour" came every afternoon when he listened to *Stella Dallas:* "I listen every afternoon—4:30 P.M. here and 1:30 P.M. on the coast. I have listened every afternoon I could for sixteen years. I once took a six-week steamship trip from New York to California and paid for a very expensive radio so that I could hear *Stella Dallas.*" These soporifics of vicarious suffering seemed to ease his own reactions.

Porter, as he said so many times, was always able to lose himself in a good dramatic show. He continued attending the premieres and performances of his own musical comedies until the last. Howard Lindsay said about him: "He was wonderful to work with. He was so enthusiastic. He would go down in the audience and laugh louder than anyone else."

But his kingdom of gaiety was beginning to dissolve around him. He had ruled the musical world of the late twenties and thirties so long—where a Porter song was the indubitable hallmark of distinction and sophistication —that he could hardly believe in the new era. The lyrical ingenunity, the amusing *risqué*, the freshness and abandon of his works had been amazing then. Now they had to give way to a new style of musical comedy. In 1943 the *Oklahoma!* of Rodgers and Hammerstein hit the boards. It was a smash from the start. Porter knew it. "The librettos are much better and the scores are much closer to the book than they used to be," he said. "They are, let us say, more musicianly." It was undoubtedly the success of *Oklahoma!* which inspired him toward his *Kiss Me, Kate* five years later.

His long and tender association with his wife (ten years older than he) was coming to an end with the first symptoms of her long illness. Linda Porter had been a legendary beauty, full of grace and dignity, radiating an almost visible sparkle of personality to light up anyone near her. Now this became dulled: she and her husband lived in separate apartments, though they saw each other every day.

More and more, between radio serials and work, his mind went back to the days when he had been the only

American in the French Foreign Legion . . . when he had sold two million sheet-music copies of "Old-Fashioned Garden" in fifteen years . . . had hired the Ballet Russe to dance in his open-air garden in Paris . . . had a villa in Bavaria and a flat in London . . . six years in Venice . . . villa in Antibes (starting the social rush there) because Linda wanted to be warm in all seasons. He fondly recalled Bali as the most civilized place on earth because "the music is fascinating and the people have reduced life to utter simplicity" . . . remembered how he used to run for exercise until his legs. . . .

In 1943 he had his own show to rival *Oklahoma!*— *Something for the Boys*. It ran for 422 performances. It was followed almost exactly a year later by *Mexican Hayride* (481 performances). *Seven Lively Arts* in December of the same year fell off sadly to 183 nights, and *Around the World in Eighty Days* (which the producer, Mike Todd, later revived for a $25,000,000 coup in motion pictures) was, in 1946, the worst failure (75 performances) yet. It took Porter two and a half years to recover from that blow. Again his wave of self-confidence ebbed out until it left his talent high and dry. Doggedly he went back to his scoring—"work means more to me than anything else"—and his career zoomed upward in a fantastic curve with *Kiss Me, Kate* and its 1,077 performances from December 30, 1948 on. *Out of This World* was a letdown again, folding after 157 performances, but the score satisfied Porter with its richness and variety of musical and lyrical invention. *Can-Can* brought him back to his customary level with 892 performances; *Silk Stockings* ran for 478 more.

But by this time even the critical notices—which he

had collected avidly for years—had ceased to interest Porter. "My valet, Paul, who has been with me for twenty years," he said, "will wake me up and either nod or shake his head." (Paul's head, he noted, had shaken only four times—*You Never Know, Seven Lively Arts, Around the World in Eighty Days, Out of This World.*) Porter grew slightly acidulous on receiving repeated requests for information on some sure-fire formulae for writing song hits. "I haven't the faintest notion of how anyone writes hits," he declared, "except for Irving Berlin, who can't help writing them." As for his own creations, he said with vigor: "God damn 'Night and Day'! Every time I write another tune, someone is bound to say that it isn't as good as 'Night and Day'!"

It may be speculation only for the ingenuous as to why he personally chose Cary Grant—handsome, over six feet (Porter was less than five-seven) to portray him in his biographical movie of 1946. But it is equally good to know it amused him that *beguine* was not only a dance but also an association of highly social medieval spinsters devoted to good works—and that *colporteur* in French meant "peddler."

His musician's curiosity and authoritative research remained as lively as ever. In 1955 he attended a party in his honor at the Waldorf, limited to his friends. The list of eight hundred had to be pruned by half in order to get the guests into the ballroom. Wan and withdrawn, holding his cane, Porter spent most of his time discussing his research into the mambo, the dance rage of the day. "There is," he said flatly, "an actual distinctive form of music in Cuba called the mambo but the craze here is such that people write songs in any tempo and call them mambos. I fully expect that the next will be called the Waltz Mambo." He paused and added slowly: "It's just something tricked up to make old people believe they are young again."

Dauntless and unchanging in his own ways, he continued to live his own life. Kate had died between the premiere of *Out of This World* and the opening of *Can-Can;* Linda between *Can-Can* and *Silk Stockings.* Those whom he knew and loved were quietly vanishing from the scene before him.

By 1954 Porter had begun his withdrawal. Most of his leisure was spent in his ivy-covered, ochre-and-black Provincial house in California. His days were passed in loincloth and white cotton robe by the pool. He wore bandages on his legs to cover the scars of the operations —they were, he felt, in as bad taste as a discussion of his income or inheritance. He had both a buzzer for summoning one of his two manservants or his housekeeper and an outdoor loudspeaker for listening to the "nondramatic suspense" of his favorite radio serials. He kept a telephone beside him, though he never took calls directly. Next to it was a small file with the numbers of his friends all over the world. "My brain is not nearly as active as it once was," he remarked, adding that the past appeared more clearly to him than the present. "That's true of everyone, I think, but particularly of myself."

Porter enjoyed hashing over the old days with occasional visitors. He recalled the time when he had taken a "beer-tour" in Germany with Woolley—tracing the brew from its lightest (Pilsener in Munich) to its darkest, an obscure liquid so thick they could scarcely swal-

Cole Porter and Mike Todd *(above)* caught in a very tense *moment* during re-hearsals of Something for the Boys. *Todd had jumped in to produce the musical after Vinton Freedley quit on it. At the right, we see Cole in what was undoubtedly a happy moment.*

Night and Day *was the motion-picture biography of Cole Porter. Cary Grant played Porter and Monty Woolley played himself.*

low it. "Both Monty and myself got so repulsively fat," he said, "that Linda refused to look at or speak to either of us until we had drastically reduced." He remembered his first interview with Louis B. Mayer, head of Metro-Goldwyn-Mayer: "He looked like a small shark."

Porter appeared to have lost his characteristic worry over his "musical success"; he declared that at times he was even happy to escape the tremendous pressure of putting out a score. But he regretted his inclination to let himself drift. "What I need," he said, "is what Ethel Barrymore once told me the wealthy retired people in Santa Barbara needed—a four-letter word. W-O-R-K." The necessary energy rarely returned. The amputation which made him a cripple ten years after his biggest triumph was the final blow.

When life left his small body in the hospital—fleeing almost before the watchers at the bedside realized it— it had the intricate simplicity of a Byronic ending: casual, useless, almost cruel, but a relief. And between the two— the classic poet and the casual music-maker—there were more than a few points of resemblance. Their disdain of society, liking for parties, contempt for blue-noses, sudden moods of withdrawal, were identical in their well-financed lives. It is not too much to borrow their *raison d'être* from a letter of Lord Byron to John Murray, his publisher, in 1821.

Said Byron: "Write to me of yourself, of the health, wealth, and welfare of all friends; but of me, little or nothing . . . send me no opinions whatsoever, either good, bad or indifferent, of yourself or your friends or others concerning any work or works of mine, past, present, or to come. . . . Opinions, good bad, or indifferent, of

97

persons in conversation or correspondence; these do not interrupt but they soil the current of my mind. . . ."

Byron added: "I want to keep my mind free and unbiassed by all paltry and personal irritabilities of praise or censure:—to let my genius take its natural direction, while my feelings are like the dead who know nothing and feel nothing of all or aught that is said or done in their regard."

Porter wanted much the same. He was too modest to claim "genius" or to dramatize himself. He had his stuffed book of clippings for his amusement while Byron had his Greek war. When the end came, Byron was sure of his place in the pantheon of poetry. Porter, working in an undeveloped medium, was never sure of his fame. He won no prizes such as the Pulitzer, nothing except the acclaim of his audiences. It is worthwhile to turn to an examination of what his status is likely to be.

FIVE

COLE PORTER BLAZED A PATH for himself through the jungle of an art that was peculiarly American and comparatively new. By the time he was tracing his infant compositions in Indiana, it was less than thirty years old—and, indeed, was not a recognizable genre at all. By the time it had firmed into its primitive patterns (about 1910), Porter was already launched on what might be called the seedbed of show music in his prep school and college careers. It was just coming into its own after World War I, and Porter was already contributing handsomely—and uniquely—to its final presence on the scene of entertainment.

All this is not to say that Porter was a pioneer or that musical comedy, as it is now known, was much more than a gathering-in of component parts which had existed for centuries. The very reason why Porter may claim to have had such a part in its creation was his love of organization, his high standards, and his adherence to his own brand of humor and high jinks, even though they brought at first nothing but disappointments. Miss Maxwell told about some of the hours devoted to comforting him (while he paid the tab) in Paris: "We used to spend long hours in all the night spots of Paris, discussing the reasons for his failures, and I remember saying to him:

" 'The reason is as plain as the nose on my face: You are too good—your standards are too high; the wit and poetry of your lyrics are beyond them (the public) and you refuse to write down to the public. But one day you will haul the public up to your own level and then the world will be yours.' "

There was more to it than that. Porter's quality of output rarely varied very much; the quality of his lyrics, despite Miss Maxwell's approval, never got much better than trickery, but his tunes were always expert, musically, and creative and inventive in their melodic line. The quantity was always there; some of his college cronies insist he hoarded most of his hits—having written them during his undergraduate years and gradually leaked them out of his trunk to Broadway producers. What caused his original turndown by the public was his refusal to act the part of a Tin Pan Alley songsmith. He recognized the genius of Irving Berlin for the popular touch and often commented wistfully upon it. His rare moments of bitterness were reserved for those whom he felt would force him to become a hack in tune writing. (It should be noted here that Berlin disagreed with Porter about writing a hit every time his fingers touched the keys. Said Berlin: "Out of more than 600 songs I have written, no more than 50 have been hits. I miss eleven times for every time I succeed.")

Beyond this, like all the others in the growing musical comedy field, Porter suffered the pains of actually creating a medium expressly to fit his talents. In this sense, it was not his failure nor that of the public but the success of the isolated tune and the incredible mélanges of nonsense that passed for entertainment. The musical comedy had to come of age—and when it did, Porter stepped directly into his rightful niche.

It is enough to point out here that musical comedy has now become one of the mainstays of the stage and is likely to remain so. It is an entertainment, in a word, intended to give pleasure to the ear, eye, and innards of an audience—while imposing minimal demands upon its mentality. In the words of the critic George Jean Nathan (himself a musical comedy addict) written in 1931, "the difference is the same difference that attaches to the mood of theatre-going in the instance of a music-show on the one hand and a dramatic play on the other. In the case of the music-show, a volitional predisposition to light pleasure and even gayety, a humor for intellect on the loose, a leaning to confetti criticism, are essential. The music-show is not for pundits in their punditical moments but for pundits, if at all, in such rare moments as they think and argue with laughter . . . (it invites one to watch) with top hat cocked saucily over his mind, with his ear filled with the hint of gay tunes, and with his eyes made merry by the imagined picture of all the relevant and appropriate clowns in the persons of actors, of madly painted canvas, and of appetizing femininity. . . ."

The world of musical comedy, like a satellite thrown off from more solid stuff, has ever had this basic relationship to music, comedy, and drama, but the manner and matter of its formation are lighter, more insubstantial, a kind of frozen effervescence. It has always meant moon travel, a drift to cloudcuckooland—in essence, a separation from self. Here it departs from opera, even from light- and folk-opera. Whereas such dramas with music endeavor to identify the audience with their themes and situations, musical comedy endeavors to set it free. It does not ask for a willing suspension of disbelief. It does not care. Its foremost symbol, one might speculate, came as early as 1905 with Eva Tanguay. She was the most un-inhibited of her sex both in vaudeville and in the Follies. She was paid $125,000 yearly (an enormous sum in those days) for the most daring acts in show business—im-provising Salome without veils, wearing forty-five-pound gowns made of coins, showing her fine legs, and shrieking her trademark song, "I Don't Care." As Miss Tanguay, the only I-Don't-Care Girl, she was paid the compliment of direct imitation and christening by the famous French musical comedy star, Mistinguette (Mees Tanguay).

Miss Tanguay never became a genuine musical comedy star—her assets were more exhibitionism than talent—but she helped set the scene for this American concoction. What resulted was a rough combination of plot and music, of costume and setting, of dialogue and diaphragm control, exercised over and smoothed out by a coopera-tive joining of musical and dramatic talents, individual in appeal yet fitting into a predetermined scheme of producer and director. What appeared to the spectator was a mass of glorious nonsense in which everything worked out improbably to the best result in the best of possible worlds. The audience left the theatre in a rosy aura, hoaxed into its momentary euphoria by the musical comedy "djinniuses." Any good musical comedy became the equivalent of an expert theatrical con game.

In his own lifetime, Porter witnessed three evolutionary changes in the chameleon styles of musical comedies. The first was *Of Thee I Sing* in 1931; the second, *Oklahoma!* in 1943; and the third, *West Side Story* in 1961. The trend was definitely toward a hard story line and a better book, less entertainment and more message, not so much glitter and glamor as sociological gilt. The old carefree attitude steadily changed toward didactic ditties and meaningful tunes. Entertainment for entertainment's sake was going out.

Porter in his personal style never paid the slightest obeisance to any of these demands. He went his own way, at his own pace—as if he were singing to himself, amusing himself with guests around the piano, not millions around the world. Traveling in Zanzibar in 1935, he had a drink in the patio of a little hotel. He found it crowded with burnoosed ivory dealers from East Africa, squatting about an old phonograph listening to a rendition of "Night and Day." "It was the greatest shock I ever had," he said, "hearing my own stuff in that out-of-the-way spot. I can't say I really liked it." He sometimes turned thumbs down on an auditioning hopeful who had selected one of his tunes as a rendition, such a performance apparently having pained him as too public a display.

All of this came about largely because Porter never lost the ability to be self-critical. Where others heard the best in what he did, he often detected the weakness. He squirmed while his nimble musical memory scurried about with ideas to patch it up. But he never went back and tinkered with his tunes, once they appeared in public and a show was going well. He preferred to drive ahead into new fields of song.

He realized that the standard which is laboriously and anxiously erected by the composer and librettist is one which depends almost wholly upon the psychological reactions of the audience. In 1883 Oscar Wilde, in writing to Marie Prescott, an American actress who played the leading part in his play *Vera, the Duchess of Padua,* a high-flown poetic bit of nonsense, said "art is the mathematical result of the emotional desire for beauty. . . . The canons of each art depend on what they appeal to. Painting appeals to the eye and is founded on the science of optics. Music appeals to the ear and is founded on the science of acoustics. The drama appeals to human nature and must have as its ultimate basis the sciences of psychology and physiology. Now, one of the facts of physiology is the desire of any very intensified emotion to be relieved by some emotion that is opposite. Nature's example is the laughter of hysteria or the tears of joy. . . . The essence of good dialogue is interruption. All good dialogue should give the effect of its being made by the reaction of the personages on one another. It should never seem to be ready-made by the author and interruptions have not only their artistic effect but their physical value. They give the actors time to breathe and get new breath power."

Though Wilde would have indignantly denied he was writing a credo for musical comedy, his words have a good deal of force in the milieu which Porter found congenial. Wilde's definition of "dialogue" is explanatory chiefly of lyrics and their usage; Porter's feeling about

104

his "lyrics" indicates that he thought of them really as musical dialogue.

In both cases, the authors were appealing to the only final judge of their art. The essence of musical comedy is what the audience is prepared to absorb, not what it is ready to accept. What pleases the eye and ear and makes for conscious enjoyment without cultural clutter (yet with some such overtones) is enough—and it is absolute. The function of a musical comedy is, basically, the art of producing happiness. It must be done in the fullness and generosity of the production, in the talent of the performers, and, most of all, in the astonishingly complex interaction of emotions within the audience itself. The post-Victorian playboys who used to buy out the whole of a performance and sit alone to enjoy it were as wretched as the actors on the stage. The audience is an indispensable part of the musical comedy; the form cannot live alone, even if it is subsidized by other sources until eternity.

Porter understood this within the framework of his own contribution. He knew its value very well; he once remarked to a friend while listening to the audience reaction to *Kiss Me, Kate:* "It's really terribly good, isn't it?" So it was. Porter was extremely flexible. He was, by all accounts, one of the great tunesmiths who was able to turn out a work of high talent and cosy composition with ease. He sometimes scribbled two or three songs for a particular part or episode and allowed someone else to select what he wanted or thought best.

It is this art of compromise which marks the best of musical comedy. There is a natural fitting together, which is the result of unnatural sweat and labor; which comes about only after infinite give-and-takes, massive re-hearsals, bouts of temperament, and fits of despair. There is a joy which emerges like iridescence to the top of the boiling pot of rivalries, jealousies, and vying talents. It is this distillation which is skimmed off by the skillful director or producer and offered to the audience as the attar of performance.

Wilde's feeling about the importance of "interruption" in dialogue is reflected by musicians' feeling about the necessity of rests in musical expression. In another definition, musical comedy might be said to be dialogue or plot interrupted by song or dance or virtuoso exhibition. The "new breath power" described by Wilde is precisely what is necessary to the whole production, to give it renewed life and zest—for if anything comes close to the controlled energy of an atomic pile in real life it is the art of musical comedy.

Yet, as has been said, such a production does not really care about art in the abstract. The whole depends upon the efficacy of the effect, however achieved. Not in vain does Porter quote his mother as saying: "Wait for the second act." It is the creed of those who know that the second act is the last in musical comedy and that the applause for the first is meaningless unless it is topped at the end. The famous quotation from Francis Quarles might be the motto of all such patient preparers:

My soul, sit thou a patient looker-on;
Judge not the play before the play is done:
Her plot hath many changes; every day
Speaks a new scene; the last act crowns the play.

Thus, in the world which Porter chose from all others and which became peculiarly his own, the fact of success is everything. But it is nothing unless it is a success which is ostensibly achieved as lightheartedly and taken as high-handedly as if it did not matter at all. And this, of course, is the essence of snobbism.

Porter deliberately chose to be a snob, at least to all appearances. He inherited money and loved it; but he made much more by himself and loved it as well. He spent it freely and gained it freely; he even complained about taxes in a lighthearted vein. "My ninety-two per cent, I suppose, supports some unknown government bureau," he said. He was determined to be a gay divorce from life and never abandoned the pose.

It was a pose. No one works as hard and revises as often—no one seeks for inspiration and chains it—no one fights for his place in the sun as desperately without being the opposite of a snob. Porter's life was a serious one—between his piano with its marked score paper and his worn rhyming dictionaries, which were always by his side. He valued the collection of a couple dozen jewelled cigarette cases given by him to his wife—one for each opening—above all other possessions, even his scores; he left them to posterity as some sort of sad symbol of what he had done.

No one can count the years that he was immersed in his work, sunk in a privacy that others took for aloofness and that he knew was necessary for creation. The land-lord of the mansion he rented for years in Brentwood told of taking away more than twenty truckloads of trees and shrubbery that had grown up or been planted by

Porter to screen himself from dilettantism. His friends complained of the "almost sinister ability" he had to detach himself and vanish from a party to do his work. Even his handwriting was that of a musician. He wrote left-handed but not horizontally—he wrote downward, one letter after another. When he relaxed, one of his pleasures was to read the biting theatre reviews of Beerbohm, that exquisite who asked and got a small place in classic critical literature.

Porter's originality did not need to be given impetus by an original story. The distinguishing traits of musical comedy had come to be that it was derivative in source and lightly satirical in tone. Great originals in the field—such as *Of Thee I Sing*—are atypical. This may be illustrated by the best representatives of musical comedy. *Oklahoma!* was derived from the play *Green Grow the Lilacs* by Lynn Riggs; *My Fair Lady* was lifted from *Pygmalion* by Shaw out of *Trilby* by du Maurier out of Greek legend; *West Side Story* was simply a modern retelling of the Romeo and Juliet legend from Shakespeare via Italian novellas. *Kiss Me, Kate*, had a similar ancestry. *Anything Goes*, another script that was hardly typical, was actually constructed (according to its rewriters, Lindsay and Crouse) around the score that Porter had already created.

Nor was much that was before this allowed to be original. In the words of Nathan, celebrating the birth of *Of Thee I Sing*, "a glance backward over the modern American musical stage will disclose it to have followed, with little deviation, routine and rusty tracks. In endless succession that stage has given us the socalled romantic musical comedies with the proud princesses in love with

humble naval lieutenants and their humble slaveys cin-
derellaed by proud princes, the revues with their vaudeville comedians and peafowl ladies, the shows laboriously
manufactured out of dull comedies previously displayed
on the legitimate stage, and the German and Austrian
importations adapted to what has been believed to be the
American taste by the insertion into their books of a
sufficient number of facetious allusions. . . . Here and
there, there has, occasionally, been a mild effort to break
away from the established pattern but the effort has been
so mild that it has come to naught and what has resulted
has been, at bottom, much the same old thing." Nathan
went on to point out that, two years previously, Kaufman, Ryskind, and Gershwin had invented a "novel
bloom" of musical comedy satire called *Strike Up the
Band* "that paved the way for the fuller and more highly
perfumed sardonic hothouse" that was *Of Thee I Sing*.

SIX

IF COLE POTER LOVED ANYTHING in this world, it was giving other people a good time. In his private life, a party was an excuse for living; in his professional career, his excuse for living was musical comedy.

He never cared very much for the opinions of those who looked down their noses at this kind of grasshopper existence. When he had inherited his portion of his grandfather's fortune, he had taken his fling at "respectable" composing with his ballet—and had given it good riddance. It has been said that "Miss Otis Regrets" (that she has a date with the hangman) was his only composition created outside musical comedy, but this is hardly true. What is true is that he never lost sight of his ambition for the stage rather than for popular hits. And his instincts for human sociability gave him a firmer basis for his art than the comments of the critics.

Indeed the ancestry of what Porter wrote may trace its right-to-be back before the beginnings of classic drama. The original meaning of "comedy" itself in the Greek—as far as it can be traced—derives from a "singing revel," presumably that of a local village. It is indissolubly connected with sex, wine, and gaiety. The earliest makeup was wine lees, rubbed on nose and cheeks to make them a comic purple. The first quips and gestures were understandably earthy. The first stage was a vineyard cart and the primitive costuming consisted largely of vine leaves. The music must have been not more than a basic beat by feet and hands and the piping of a *nay* or syrinx.

Aristophanes, with his scatological comedy and choruses, was probably the first formally to write such material—what Porter later called, referring to *The New Yorkers* in 1930, "sociological musical satire." For centuries drama was invariably presented with music and lyrics and comic turns. *The Tempest* and a dozen other works of Shakespeare may be held within these bounds without much exaggeration. The masques and antimasques of Ben Jonson and Inigo Jones were purely musical comedy—with their casts drawn from the court and their budgets quite comparable to those of Broadway in modern times. Their production of *Love's Welcome* for Charles I, a magnificent masque given in the king's honor at Bolsover Castle by the Duke of Newcastle, cost 14,000 pounds. Granting conservatively that the worth of the pound since—in services, costumes, materials, and mechanical effects—has fallen off at least twelve times in three hundred years, the total expense of such a stunning presentation today would be more than $840,000.

The rise of musical comedy as a specific facet of

entertainment, however, may be largely credited to the United States. The story of this art is one of the most confused evolutionary histories of the theatre. Any survey must deal with native and imported specimens and their offshoots. It must include vaudeville, variety, *opéra bouffe*, opera (heavy), and opera (light). It must cover operetta, revue, follies, whirl, antic, gambol, revel, scandal, ballet, comic opera, farce opera, spectacle, pantomime, minstrel show, and a score of others. All of these figure in one way or another in the final issue.

But its date of inception, gradual as it was, may safely be settled as post-Civil War. *The Black Crook* of 1866 has been generally given as the first such performance but this, with its French ballet, German melodrama, two hundred female legs, and rich staging was rather the last of the old spectacles. The first presentation which can safely be identified was the production of *Evangeline* in 1874, a satire upon Longfellow's well-known poem. The authors, Edward Rice and J. Cheever Goodwin, called it first an "opera-bouffe," then an "extravaganza," and finally hit upon the term "musical comedy." Goodwin (an ex-reporter) wrote the book and Rice devised the music—playing the piano by ear and transcribing it into a script no one but he could decipher. In his later shows, Rice "dictated" the musical "effects" that he wanted and let someone else arrange them in palatable musical form. No one knows how many performances the first version of *Evangeline* had, but a revival in 1885 ran 251 nights in New York alone. The year before that, Rice brought out *Adonis*, a "burlesque-extravaganza" with dialogue rewritten weekly to keep up with news of the day. It ran for 603 consecutive nights. Goodwin appeared again in

...ver fully recovered ...er his riding accident, ...rter made every effort ...walk under his own ...wer.

1891 with a show called *Wang*, laid in Siam with lines such as the king's: "I don't reign, I sprinkle." For the first time such an "operatic burletta" had an excellent composer, Woolson Morse (competent enough to be asked by W. S. Gilbert to collaborate with him after the latter's split with Sullivan). The coming dependence on Shakespeare as a source was anticipated in 1894 by a show called Hamlet II—in which Laertes, Rosencrantz, Guildenstern, Osric, and Hamlet all appeared as dainty damsels in tights doing exotic dances. Five years later the first of the unending Jules Verne burlesques popped up, *Around New York in Eighty Minutes.*

Floradora came in 1900 and achieved its fame on the basis of its six matched girls—each 130 pounds, five-foot-four, brunette or redheaded. The show ran 505 performances (after a year in London) but its book and music were remarkably thin. *The Wizard of Oz* was noteworthy chiefly because of its expert staging in 1903; Victor Herbert's music in *Babes in Toyland*, the same year, was equally noteworthy—as were *Mlle. Modiste*, in 1905, and a rapid succession of others. The Irish-born, English-bred, German-trained, American success that was bound up in Herbert marked the first ascent to musical integrity in musical comedy.

A review in the *Dramatic Mirror* commented in 1907 that in musical comedy "nothing but the expected happens: choruses sing, dance, stand in line, smile, wear colored clothes; principals get into trouble and out of it, burst into songs at intervals commensurate with their importance, make jokes about New York, do specialities of more or less cleverness; the curtain falls to divide the evening into two parts; the orchestra plays the air that the promoter hopes will be popular. The whole thing is done according to formula as accurately as a prescription is compounded in a drug store. And the audience, strictly ritualistic as a musical comedy audience always is, is pleased."

It was a summing up which was not to stand for long. True, the old style had its way a little longer. *The Merry Widow* of 1907 (with its excellent Franz Lehar score) did little but romanticize the atmosphere for 416 performances; the *Ziegfeld Follies* of the same year glamorized it. But there appeared a fresh spirit, in the person of George M. Cohan. Despite the invariable thinness of his book and music, under the frown of the critics, his very mugging and brashness had an enormous audience appeal. His productions showed speed and breeziness; they modernized the stilted language of the old shows and demonstrated clearly the shape of things to come. *The Pink Lady* of 1911 began to suit both critics and public with an "amusing book and pleasing music, a rare combination." Herbert, of course, continued to be king of the era, turning out five smash hits and eight lesser shows in the six years before 1917. But in 1912 his rival, Rudolf Friml, with an expert writer, Otto Hauerbach, put on *The Firefly* to begin a career as auspicious and successful as that of Herbert.

There were inevitable lapses into the past. *Sumurun* in 1912 was a ponderous German fantasy import; *Chu Chin Chow*, an imitation, was as much of an artistic dud as a commercial success in 1914. Nevertheless, portents began to show. In 1912 *The Red Petticoat* appeared with a score by Jerome Kern, a young man who had spent eight years in Broadway musical apprenticeship. Not even the appearance of *The Sunshine Girl* in 1913, a sentimental throwback that created the term "soap opera," could withstand the onrush of the future; nor could the revival of revues and elaborate spectacles, with their nostalgic comics and beautiful girls, hold it back.

Wars have always affected popular choices in the theatre. World War I and musical comedy were no exception. At the end of 1914, a completely new kind of musical comedy appeared with music and lyrics by Irving Berlin. *Watch Your Step* was a "syncopated musical show" complete with ragtime and jazz, including a hopped-up version of the famed Rigoletto quartette. It was a sound success, running for 175 performances. What was even more significant was that the next month, in January, 1915, Jerome Kern made his first full-dress debut of talent with *Ninety in the Shade*. However, it ran only for forty performances, even though it had an assist from a new writer, Guy Bolton, who did a literate book. Kern wrote four shows that year. The third, called *Very Good, Eddie*, was produced by Elizabeth Marbury (who was to produce Porter's first fiasco). It had an astonishing 341 performances. Both its plot and dialogue were coherent and convincing, derived from a Broadway stage farce. Bolton, who did musical comedy "books" from then on, had expressed the belief that the public wanted realism in the plot. Success should depend, he said, "as much on plot and character development for success as on the music." In his *Oh, Boy!* (1917) he began to overthrow the standard romantic conception: it was, he said, the first musical comedy written as a "straight consistent comedy with the addition of music. Every song and lyric contributed to the action. The humor was based on situation, not inter-jected by the comedians." If Bolton was talking about strictly modern American musical comedy, he may have been right. But the choruses of Aristophanes surely advanced the plot; and *The Beggar's Opera* of 1728 (much more of a musical comedy than an "opera"), with its extraordinary sixty-two performances, was the first to integrate wholly music, lyrics, and action.

It was obviously high time for Cole Porter to make his entrance from the wings. He was out of Yale, fresh out of Harvard, and had his trunk packed full of songs that no one would use. He haunted the dazzling world of Broadway and took in the exciting air of a new form just beginning to take over its own. The book had as-sumed the tough resiliency he could use; the music was reaching for higher standards; the lyrics made sense. What this shy twenty-five-year-old could add to it, he was not sure. But *See America First* resulted in Porter's being last seen for three years. By the time he got back from his self-imposed exile, spirits restored, the scene had changed again.

The long delay from this point on in Porter's career does not seem to be wholly explained by his own feeling that he was rejected by the producers. Five years elapsed between *Hitchy-Koo* and the *Greenwich Village Follies* of 1924; four more elapsed before the opening of *Paris* and the real launching of his career. This nine-year hiatus cannot be attributed to failure. Hitchcock's revue was a break-even thing and, although the days when a hundred performances of a show represented a handsome profit were passing, the *Follies* was certainly a respectable success.

Part of the delay was due to Porter's having too much of a good time. He was subsidized by his friends, his wife, and his mother. He loved travel and new acquaintances; his ego was on the build. He simply did not try too hard and here perhaps he was right. He needed time for the Indiana farm-boy to be submerged in the worldly wise sophisticate. He felt he needed to study more music. His feelings of inadequacy returned after the *Follies*. They did not vanish until 1928.

There were other factors at work as well. The musical comedy world had not been at a standstill while Porter made up his mind. On the contrary, it had been going ahead at a breakneck pace with all sorts of innovations—most of which led directly toward the past. Above everyone else towered the figure of Ziegfeld. He hired Berlin, Herbert, and Friml; he induced Hitchcock, Porter's first sponsor, to leave off his productions and work for him. Stars of every sort flocked to work under his opulent direction. Mistinguette had appeared and been sent back to Paris with derogatory critical notices not unlike those of her namesake twenty years before. A supremely assured youngster, George Gershwin, had appeared the same year as Porter to do tunes for the *Morris Gest Midnight Whirl*, writing items like "Cutie, Cut Your Cuticle."

Another song-writing team, Richard Rodgers and Lorenz Hart, appeared with the *Garrick Gaieties*—a Theatre Guild spoof of everything available—in 1925. A British import, *André Charlot's Revue*, had succeeded very well the year before with a fresh talent named Noel Coward. These had taken their cue from the revues which were in the advanced stages of naughtiness and nudity. But the development of the musical comedy had not advanced an inch. One, *Arabesque*, proffered a scene where a "Bedouin girl, dressed down to the utmost finesse of nakedness, straddles a sheik, who lies full-length on a cloak on the floor of a savage tent at midnight, alone with her."

Herbert was on his inevitable decline. Friml was on the rise to his saccharine *The Vagabond King* of 1925. He was rivalled by a newcomer named Sigmund Romberg with *The Student Prince* (1924). Kern seemed to be under wraps, occasionally producing songs like "Look for the Silver Lining." Berlin appeared to have lost his first fine burst of creativity, devoting his time to hack revue work—his best being a score for *The Cocoanuts* (1925) and the Marx Brothers. Gershwin alone produced sound work in *Lady, Be Good* (1924) and *Tell Me More* (1925), efforts that upheld the new standards.

Other names such as Ray Henderson, Lew Brown, Buddy de Sylva, and Vincent Youmans (whom Porter admired greatly and imitated to some extent) appeared on the playbills. But still it was Gershwin who continued to lead the van with *Oh, Kay* (1926) and *Funny Face* (1927). It was he, together with his brother Ira and Morrie Ryskind, who concocted the first really great and original musical comedy, *Strike Up the Band*, in 1930. Concerning it, that discerning critic William Bolitho wrote: "I don't remember ever before in a musical comedy having noticed or understood what it was all about. Here all is not only clear but really startling. Of all things in the world, here is a bitter, rather good, satirical attack on war, genuine propaganda at times, sung and danced on Broadway, to standing room only."

Strike Up the Band lacked nothing and found complete public acceptance. The era of improbable sweetness and light was over. The stage was set for the emergence and gradual evolution of Porter's craft which was to dominate the last of the twenties and most of the thirties, coming to its crescendo in the last of the forties.

SEVEN

HERE AT LAST COLE PORTER can be located in the world of musical comedy. Enough time has elapsed so that he may be seen clearly as what he was. It must be confessed at once that he was not original. He was deeply influenced by his times, by his colleagues in song writing, by the styles of the stage, by his acquisition of melody and rhythm on his travels. But Shakespeare had only one original plot out of thirty-nine plays and he never had to do with the frantic whims of musical comedy producers. An accusation of lack of originality is not an unduly serious charge against musical comedy artists. The imposition of tune and choreography, of wit and gaiety, upon a solid substratum of derivative story is almost a necessary reassurance to the audience— the enjoyment of something dimly familiar.

Nor can it be held against Porter that he was not serious. Satire, used as Jonathan Swift used it, may become a malign and destroying influence. This was far from Porter's intention: he preferred the fencing touch rather than cutlass and bludgeon. He did not even aspire to the home thrust; he preferred to flutter from flower to flower of inanity and leave only a momentary sting. It is possibly significant that his most skillful gift for the satiric point lies in his concepts of sexual relationships.

It is undeniable that he had a transforming effect upon his melding of words and music. As his friend Moss Hart said: "No one could write a Cole Porter song but Cole Porter. Each song had a design and a special felicity of its own that stamped it as uniquely his." He was inimitable. He had no disciples and wanted none.

Ten years after his first real success, Porter was acknowledged as an outstanding writer of musical comedy. He stuck to his last and never tried to alter the librettos. "Words and music are quite enough of a job," he said. He had achieved not only leadership, he had achieved innovation. His work had shifted musical comedy onto new and higher ground. He was, as one of his friends said, "a new musical voice of immense vigor and freshness . . . a forcible talent that was racy and bold but that had great elegance and a curious kind of purity." Another declared "he was to our generation what Gilbert and Sullivan were to theirs. His satire is just as merciless and he, too, hides the face of a philosopher and reformer behind the gay mask of a royal entertainer." Still another put it in the way that Porter might have liked best of all: "Cole knew more about the art of living than anyone else I've ever known. . . . He had a wonderful, wonderful sense of gaiety."

The critics were more analytical. One, Cecil Smith, pointed out that "he made use of satirically-oriented books but preferred to employ as his weapon the barbed shaft of an individual line or song. . . . He developed his technique of acid comment only slowly, contenting himself at first with a special urbanity of manner. . . . A *mot* or turn of phrase always meant more to him than anything else about his work; give him a choice between sacrificing the integrity of a character and sacrificing a rhyme and he would unhesitatingly sacrifice the character. He always was . . . primarily a *litterateur* and genteel pornographer."

The bluntness of this appraisal must be tempered somewhat with the judgment of Sigmund Spaeth, writing in 1948 just before Porter's ultimate triumph of *Kiss Me, Kate.* He described Porter as "our most literate and sophisticated creator of popular songs . . . (showing) equal facility with text and tune, developing the two simultaneously in seemingly inevitable fashion. His only rivals in this respect are Irving Berlin and Stephen Foster himself. The group of trained musicians . . . beginning with Victor Herbert and including such names as Kern, Gershwin, Friml, Romberg, and Rodgers, can well single out Cole Porter as perhaps the most individual of them all. How he could turn out such a vast literature under the handicaps of his way of life remains an eternal mystery. He seems to have the power of absolute concentration, thinking out a complete composition, regardless of his surroundings, without going near a piano or a piece of music-paper."

Possibly the first summary is a little too harsh and the second is a little too generous. What they do is to illustrate the extremes of appreciation in which Porter was held. The upshot of it must be that throughout his life the composer dared to be himself, a person capable both of sentiment and scintillation, but always unique.

Cole Porter trusted his best self. He played his own part and spoke his message of music under his own name in his own way. He related it, without hesitation, to the style of his own day (which he molded into his own image) and made it correspond to the needs of the musical comedy art. He drew upon his life and experiences for its sustenance and operated in the milieu without the thought of an apology. Musical comedy was good enough for him; the only question in his mind was that he himself might not be good enough for it. He preached a gospel of detachment and hovered behind it. Nothing in this world was quite worth the winning: it was the work of the moment that was savory, that mattered.

What will make his creations live and thrive—as they have already proven—is their cool, wry objectivity. They have no special flavor, rather a kind of temperature and a dash of spice, a musical glass of cold water on an emotionally hot day. Because they really suit no one but Porter they have the facility of fitting everyone over the years. When Bianca, in *Kiss Me, Kate*, sings that "I never yet beheld that special face which I could fancy more than any other," she is singing Porter's own epitaph —and the universal reason why his fragile monument will stand.

BIBLIOGRAPHY

BIBLIOGRAPHY

COLE PORTER SONGS
REGISTERED FOR COPYRIGHT

Abracadabra, Chappell & Co., Inc., 1944
Ace in the Hole, Chappell & Co., Inc., 1941
Adios Argentina, Harms, Inc., 1935
After You, Harms, Inc., 1932
Aladdin, Cole Porter, 1957
All I've Got To Get Now Is My Man, Chappell & Co.,
   Inc., 1940
All of You, Cole Porter, 1954
All Through the Night, Harms, Inc., 1934
Allez-Vous-En, Cole Porter, 1952
Almiro, Harms, Inc., 1928
Alone with You, Herman Darewski Music Pub. Co.,
   1918
Altogether Too Fond of You, Herman Darewski Music
   Pub. Co., 1918
Always True to You in My Fashion, Cole Porter, 1948
The American Punch, Harms, Inc., 1922

125

Another Op'nin', Another Show, Cole Porter, 1949

Another Sentimental Song, T. B. Harms and Francis, Day & Hunter, 1919

Anything Goes, Harms, Inc., 1934

Aphrodite's Dance, Harms, Inc., 1935

Aqua Sincopada, Harms, Inc., 1929

As on Through the Seasons We Sail, Cole Porter, 1954

At Last in Your Arms, Loew's, Inc., 1939

At Long Last Love, Chappell & Co., Inc., 1937

The Band Started Swinging a Song, Chappell & Co., Inc., 1945

The Bandit Band, Chappell & Co., Ltd., 1922

The Banjo That Man Joe Plays, Harms, Inc., 1929

Be a Clown, Chappell & Co., Inc., 1946

Begin the Beguine, Harms, Inc., 1935

Between You and Me, Chappell & Co., Inc., 1939

Bianca, Cole Porter, 1948

Bianca's Theme, Cole Porter, 1949

Bingo Eli Yale, Jerome H. Remick & Co., 1910

Blow, Gabriel, Blow, Harms, Inc., 1934

The Blue Boy Blues, Chappell & Co., Ltd., 1922

Bobolink Waltz, Cole Porter, 1902

Boogie Barcarolle, Chappell & Co., Inc., 1941

Bridget, Cole Porter, 1910

Bring Me Back My Butterfly, T. B. Harms and Francis, Day & Hunter, 1919

Brittany, Harms, Inc., 1924

Brush Up Your Shakespeare, Cole Porter, 1949

Buddie Beware, Harms, Inc., 1934

But He Never Says He Loves Me, Cole Porter, 1930

But in the Morning No, Chappell & Co., Inc., 1939

Buy Her a Box at the Opera, G. Schirmer, 1916

By—Candlelight, Chappell & Co., Inc., 1938
By the Mississinewah, Chappell & Co., Inc., 1943
Ça, C'est l'amour, Buxton Hill Music Corp., 1956
Calypso, Buxton Hill Music Corp., 1956
Can-Can, Cole Porter, 1952
Carlotta, Chappell & Co., Inc., 1944
Caroline, Loew's, Inc., 1955
C'est Magnifique, Cole Porter, 1952
Cherry Pies Ought To Be You, Cole Porter, 1950
The Chiripah, Harms, Inc., 1935
Climb up the Mountain, Cole Porter, 1950
Close, Chappell & Co., Inc., 1937
Cocktail Time, Chappell & Co., Ltd., 1922
Come Along with Me, Cole Porter, 1953
Come On In, Chappell & Co., Inc., 1940
Come to the Supermarket in Old Peking, Cole Porter, 1958
Could It Be You?, Chappell & Co., Inc., 1942
Count Your Blessings, Chappell & Co., Inc., 1944
The Crew Song, Cole Porter, 1953
De-Lovely, Chappell & Co., Inc., 1936
Do I Love You?, Chappell & Co., Inc., 1939
Don't Fence Me In, Harms, Inc., 1944
Don't Look at Me That Way, Harms, Inc., 1928
Down in the Depths, Chappell & Co., Inc., 1936
Dream Dancing, Chappell & Co., Inc., 1941
Drinking Song, Loew's, Inc., 1956
Easy to Love, Chappell & Co., Inc., 1936
The Elizabethan Club, Cole Porter, 1953
Entrance of Juno, Cole Porter, 1951
Eric, Harms, Inc., 1935
Esmerelda, Irving Berlin, Inc., 1915

Ever and Ever Yours, G. Schirmer, 1916

Ev-rybod-ee Who's Anybod-ee, Harms, Inc., 1935

Ev'ry Day a Holiday, Chappell & Co., Inc., 1940

Ev'ry Man Is a Stupid Man, Cole Porter, 1953

Ev'rything I Love, Chappell & Co., Inc., 1941

Ev'ry Time We Say Goodbye, Chappell & Co., Inc., 1944

Experiment, Harms, Inc., 1933

Far Away, Chappell & Co., Inc., 1938

Farewell, Amanda, Buxton Hill Music Co., 1949

Farming, Chappell & Co., Inc., 1941

Fated To Be Mated, Buxton Hill Music Co., 1956

Feathermore, Harms, Inc., 1935

Find Me a Primitive Man, Harms, Inc., 1929

First Act Finale ("Kiss Me, Kate"), Cole Porter, 1949

A Fool There Was, Metro-Goldwyn-Mayer Corp., 1936

For No Rhyme or Reason, Chappell & Co., Inc., 1938

Frahngee-Pahnee, Chappell & Co., Inc., 1944

Fresh as a Daisy, Chappell & Co., Inc., 1940

Friendship, Chappell & Co., Inc., 1939

From—Alpha—to—Omega, Chappell & Co., Inc., 1938

From Now On, Chappell & Co., Inc., 1938

From This Moment On, Cole Porter, 1950

Get Out of Town, Chappell & Co., Inc., 1938

Girls, Chappell & Co., Inc., 1944

Les Girls, Buxton Hill Music Corp., 1956

Give Him the Oo-la-la, Chappell & Co., Inc., 1940

Glide, Glider, Glide, Army Air Forces Aid Society, 1943

Good-Bye, Little Dream, Good-Bye, Chappell & Co., Inc., 1936

Good Morning, Miss Standing, Harms, Inc., 1935

The Good-Will Movement, Chappell & Co., Inc., 1943

The Great Indoors, Harms, Inc., 1930
Gypsy in Me, Harms, Inc., 1934
Hail Bibinski, Cole Porter, 1955
Hans, Harms, Inc., 1928
The Happy Heaven of Harlem, Harms, Inc., 1929
The Harbor Deep Down in My Heart, Harms, Inc., 1922
Hark to the Song of the Night, Cole Porter, 1950
Hasta Luego, Chappell & Co., Inc., 1942
The Heaven Hop, Harms, Inc., 1928
Hence, It Don't Make Sense, Chappell & Co., Inc., 1944
Her Heart Was in Her Work, Cole Porter, 1952
Here Comes the Band Wagon, Harms, Inc., 1929
He's a Right Guy, Chappell & Co., Inc., 1942
Hey, Babe, Hey, Chappell & Co., Inc., 1936
Hey, Good-Lookin', Chappell & Co., Inc., 1942
High Flyin' Wings of My Shoes, Loew's, Inc., 1957
High Society Calypso, Loew's, Inc., 1955
Hot-House Rose, Harms, Inc., 1954
How Could We Be Wrong?, Harms, Inc., 1933
How's Your Romance?, Harms, Inc., 1932
Hush, Hush, Hush, Cole Porter, 1949
I Adore You, Cole Porter, 1957
I Always Knew, Chappell & Co., Inc., 1942
I Am in Love, Cole Porter, 1952
I Am in Love Again, Harms, Inc., 1925
I Am Loved, Cole Porter, 1949
I Concentrate on You, Chappell & Co., Inc., 1939
I Do, Cole Porter, 1952
I Dream of a Girl in a Shawl, Harms, Inc., 1929
I Get a Kick out of You, Harms, Inc., 1934
I Got Beauty, Cole Porter, 1951
I Happen to Be in Love, Chappell & Co., Inc., 1939

I Happen to Like New York, Harms, Inc., 1931

I Hate Men, Cole Porter, 1948

I Hate You, Darling, Chappell & Co., Inc., 1941

I Introduced, T. B. Harms and Francis, Day & Hunter, 1919

I Jupiter, Cole Porter, 1949

I Know It's Not Meant for Me, Metro-Goldwyn-Mayer Corp., 1937

I Love Paris, Cole Porter, 1952

I Love You, Chappell & Co., Inc., 1943

I Love You, Samantha, Buxton Hill Music Corp., 1955

I Loved Him but He Didn't Love Me, Harms, Inc., 1929

I Never Realized (Lyrics only), Leo Feist, Inc., 1921

I Shall Positively Pay You Next Monday, Cole Porter, 1952

I Sing of Love, Cole Porter, 1949

I Sleep Easier Now, Cole Porter, 1951

I Want to Be Raided by You, Harms, Inc., 1929

I Want to Go Home, Chappell & Co., Inc., 1938

I Worship You, Harms, Inc., 1929

If You Loved Me Truly, Cole Porter, 1953

If You Smile at Me, Chappell & Co., Inc., 1946

I'm a Gigolo, Harms, Inc., 1929

I'm Ashamed That Women Are So Simple, Cole Porter, 1948

I'm Getting Myself Ready for You, Harms, Inc., 1930

I'm in Love, Harms, Inc., 1929

I'm in Love with a Soldier Boy, Chappell & Co., Inc., 1943

I'm So in Love with You, Loew's, Inc., 1939

I'm Unlucky at Gambling, and I'm Unlucky at Love, Harms, Inc., 1929

In Hitchy's Garden, T. B. Harms and Francis, Day & Hunter, 1919

In the Still of the Night, Chappell & Co., Inc., 1937

Is It the Girl? (Or Is It the Gown?), Chappell & Co., Inc., 1944

It All Belongs to You, Chappell & Co., Inc., 1938

It Might Have Been, Chappell & Co., Inc., 1942

It Must Be Fun to Be You, Chappell & Co., Inc., 1943

It Was Written in the Stars, Chappell & Co., Inc., 1939

It's a Chemical Reaction, That's All, Cole Porter, 1954

It's All Over but the Shouting, Metro-Goldwyn-Mayer Corp., 1937

It's All Right with Me, Cole Porter, 1953

It's Bad for Me, Harms, Inc., 1933

I've a Shooting Box in Scotland, G. Schirmer, 1916

I've a Strange New Rhythm in My Heart, Chappell & Co., Inc., 1937

I've Come to Wive It Wealthily in Padua, Cole Porter, 1949

I've Got an Awful Lot to Learn, G. Schirmer, 1916

I've Got My Eyes on You, Chappell & Co., Inc., 1939

I've Got Somebody Waiting, T. B. Harms and Francis, Day & Hunter, 1919

I've Got You on My Mind, Harms, Inc., 1932

I've Got You Under My Skin, Chappell & Co., Inc., 1936

I've Still Got My Health, Chappell & Co., Inc., 1940

Jerry, My Soldier Boy, Chappell & Co., Inc., 1942

Josephine, Cole Porter, 1955

Just One of Those Things, Harms, Inc., 1930

Katie Went to Haiti, Chappell & Co., Inc., 1939

The Kling Kling Bird, Harms, Inc., 1935

Ladies in Waiting, Loew's, Inc., 1956

Lady Fair, Harms, Inc., 1935

The Language of Flowers (Collaboration with T. Lawrason Riggs), G. Schirmer, 1916

The Law, Cole Porter, 1952

The Laziest Gal in Town, Cole Porter, 1927

The Leader of a Big-Time Band, Chappell & Co., Inc., 1943

Let's Be Buddies, Chappell & Co., Inc., 1940

Let's Do It, Harms, Inc., 1947

Let's Do It, Let's Fall in Love, Harms, Inc., 1928

Let's Fly Away, Harms, Inc., 1930

Let's Misbehave, Harms, Inc., 1927

Let's Not Talk about Love, Chappell & Co., Inc., 1941

Let's Step Out, Harms, Inc., 1930

Let's Vocalize, Loew's, Inc., 1955

Lima (Collaboration with T. Lawrason Riggs), G. Schirmer, 1916

Little One, Buxton Hill Music Corp., 1955

A Little Rumba Numba, Chappell & Co., Inc., 1941

A Little Skipper from Heaven Above, Chappell & Co., Inc., 1936

Live and Let Live, Chappell & Co., Inc., 1952

Look Around (Words by Clifford Grey), Chappell & Co., Ltd., 1920

Look What I Found, Chappell & Co., Inc., 1946

Looking at You, Harms, Inc., 1929

Lotus-Bloom, Chappell & Co., Inc., 1942

Love for Sale, Harms, Inc., 1930

Love Letter Words, Harms, Inc., 1922

Love Me, Love My Pekinese, Chappell & Co., Inc., 1936

Love of My Life, Chappell & Co., Inc., 1946

Mack, The Black, Chappell & Co., Inc., 1946

Make Ev'ry Day a Holiday, Harms, Inc., 1924

Make It Another Old Fashioned, Please, Chappell & Co., Inc., 1940

Make Way, Cole Porter, 1958

Manuela, Loew's, Inc., 1946

Maria, Chappell & Co., Inc., 1938

Me and Marie, Harms, Inc., 1935

Military Maids, Harms, Inc., 1928

Mind If I Make Love to You?, Buxton Hill Music Corp., 1955

Miss Otis Regrets She's Unable to Lunch Today, Harms, Inc., 1934

Mister and Missus Fitch, Harms, Inc., 1954

Mr. and Mrs. Smith, Harms, Inc., 1935

Monmart', Cole Porter, 1952

Most Gentlemen Don't Like Love, Chappell & Co., Inc., 1938

My Barcelona Maid, Chappell & Co., Inc., 1941

My Cozy Little Corner in the Ritz, T. B. Harms and Francis, Day & Hunter, 1919

My Heart Belongs to Daddy, Chappell & Co., Inc., 1938

My Long Ago Girl, Harms, Inc., 1924

My Lou-Lou, Harms, Inc., 1935

My Most Intimate Friend, Harms, Inc., 1935

My Mother Would Love You, Chappell & Co., Inc., 1940

National Anthem, Metro-Goldwyn-Mayer Corp., 1937

Never Give Anything Away, Cole Porter, 1952

Never, Never Be an Artist, Cole Porter, 1953

Night and Day, Harms, Inc., 1932

Nina, Chappell & Co., Inc., 1946

No Lover, Cole Porter, 1949

No Wonder Taxes Are High, Cole Porter, 1958

Nobody's Chasing Me, Cole Porter, 1949

Now You Has Jazz, Buxton Hill Music Corp., 1955

Nymph Errant, Harms, Inc., 1933

Oh, Bright, Fair Dream, G. Schirmer, 1916

Old Fashioned Garden, T. B. Harms and Francis, Day & Hunter, 1919

Old-Fashioned Girl, Harms, Inc., 1928

Olga Come Back to the Volga, Chappell & Co., Ltd., 1922

Only Another Boy and Girl, Chappell & Co., Inc., 1944

Opening Act 1 Scene 1, Cole Porter, 1952

Opening Laundry Scene, Cole Porter, 1952

Opening—Romanza Sequence, Metro-Goldwyn-Mayer Corp., 1937

Opening to Beach Scene, Harms, Inc., 1935

Opportunity Knocks but Once, Cole Porter, 1957

Our Crown, Harms, Inc., 1935

Our Hotel (Words by Clifford Grey), Chappell & Co., Ltd., 1920

Ours, Chappell & Co., Inc., 1936

The Ozarks Are Callin' Me Home, Chappell & Co., Inc., 1936

Paree What Did You Do To Me?, Harms, Inc., 1929

Paris, Harms, Inc., 1928

Paris Loves Lovers, Cole Porter, 1954

Perennial Debutantes, Chappell & Co., Inc., 1936

Peter Piper, T. B. Harms and Francis, Day & Hunter, 1919

The Physician (But He Never Said He Loved Me), Harms, Inc., 1933

A Picture of Me Without You, Harms, Inc., 1935

Pipe Dreaming, Chappell & Co., Inc., 1946

Pity Me Please, G. Schirmer, 1916

Please Don't Make Me Be Good, Harms, Inc., 1929

Please Don't Monkey with Broadway, Loew's, Inc., 1939

Prithee, Come Crusading with Me (Collaboration with T. Lawrason Riggs), G. Schirmer, 1916

The Queen of Terre Haute, Harms, Inc., 1929

Quelque-Chose, Harms, Inc., 1927

The Ragtime Pipes of Pan, Ascherberg, Hopwood & Crew, Ltd., 1922

Rap Tap on Wood, Chappell & Co., Inc., 1936

The Red Blues, Cole Porter, 1955

Red, Hot and Blue, Chappell & Co., Inc., 1936

Ridin' High, Chappell & Co., Inc., 1936

The Ritz Roll and Rock, Loew's, Inc., 1956

River God, Chappell & Co., Inc., 1938

Rolling Home, Chappell & Co., Inc., 1936

Rosalie, Chappell & Co., Inc., 1937

Rub Your Lamp, Chappell & Co., Inc., 1941

Sailors of the Sky, Chappell & Co., Inc., 1943

Satin and Silk, Cole Porter, 1954

Second Act—Shrew Finale, Cole Porter, 1949

See America First (Collaboration with T. Lawrason Riggs), G. Schirmer, 1916

See That You're Born in Texas, Chappell & Co., Inc., 1943

Shootin' the Works for Uncle Sam, Chappell & Co., Inc., 1941

Should I Tell You I Love You?, Chappell & Co., Inc., 1946

Siberia, Cole Porter, 1954

The Sidecar, Harms, Inc., 1935

Silk Stockings, Cole Porter, 1954

Since I Kissed My Baby Goodbye, Chappell & Co., Inc., 1941

Sing Jubilee, Harms, Inc., 1935

Sing to Me Guitar, Chappell & Co., Inc., 1944

Six Little Wives, Harms, Inc., 1935

Slow Sinks the Sun (Collaboration with T. Lawrason Riggs), G. Schirmer, 1916

So in Love, Cole Porter, 1948

So Near and Yet So Far, Chappell & Co., Inc., 1941

Solomon, Harms, Inc., 1933

Something for the Boys, Chappell & Co., Inc., 1942

Something to Shout About, Chappell & Co., Inc., 1942

Something's Got To Be Done (Collaboration with T. Lawrason Riggs), G. Schirmer, 1916

The Sponge, Chappell & Co., Ltd., 1922

Spring Love Is in the Air, Metro-Goldwyn-Mayer Corp., 1937

Step Montage A, Loew's, Inc., 1956

Stereophonic Sound, Cole Porter, 1955

Sunday Morning Breakfast Time, Harms, Inc., 1935

Swing That Swing, Harms, Inc., 1935

Swingin' the Jinx Away, Chappell & Co., Inc., 1936

Take Me back to Manhattan, Harms, Inc., 1930

Taking the Steps to Russia, Chappell & Co., Inc., 1938

Tarantella, Cole Porter, 1949

Thank You so Much Missus Lowsborough—Goodby, Harms, Inc., 1934

That Black and White Baby of Mine, T. B. Harms and Francis, Day and Hunter, 1919

There He Goes Mister Phileas Fogg, Chappell & Co., Inc., 1946

There Must Be Some One for Me, Chappell & Co., Inc., 1944

There'll Always Be a Lady Fair, Harms, Inc., 1936

There's Nothing Like Swimming, Harms, Inc., 1935

They All Fall in Love, Harms, Inc., 1929

They Couldn't Compare to You, Cole Porter, 1951

To Get Away, Harms, Inc., 1935

To Love or Not to Love, Metro-Goldwyn-Mayer Corp., 1937

To Think That This Could Happen to Me, Cole Porter, 1952

Tom, Dick or Harry, Cole Porter, 1949

To-morrow, Chappell & Co., Inc., 1938

Tonight I Love You More Than Ever Before, Cole Porter, 1949

Too Bad, Cole Porter, 1955

Too Darn Hot, Cole Porter, 1949

True Love, Buxton Hill Music Corp., 1955

Trust Your Destiny to Your Star, Cole Porter, 1957

Two Big Eyes (Words by John L. Golden), T. B. Harms and Francis, Day & Hunter, 1915

Two Little Babes in the Wood, Harms, Inc., 1928

Use Your Imagination, Cole Porter, 1949

Visit Panama, Chappell & Co., Inc., 1940

Vivienne, Harms, Inc., 1928

Voodoo, Chappell & Co., Inc., 1946

Wait for the Moon, Harms, Inc., 1924

Wake Up and Dream, Harms, Inc., 1929

Waltz Down the Aisle, Harms, Inc., 1934

Washington Square (Lyrics by Porter and E. Ray Goetz;

music by Melville Gideon), Jerome H. Remick & Co., 1920

We Are Maidens Typical of France, Cole Porter, 1953

We Open in Venice, Cole Porter, 1949

We Shall Never Be Younger, Cole Porter, 1955

The Wedding Cake Walk, Chappell & Co., Inc., 1941

Well, Did you Evah?, Chappell & Co., Inc., 1940

Were Thine That Special Face, Cole Porter, 1948

Weren't We Fools?, Harms, Inc., 1927

What a Crazy Way to Spend Sunday, Chappell & Co., Inc., 1944

What a Fair Thing Is a Woman, Cole Porter, 1952

What a Great Pair We'll Be, Chappell & Co., Inc., 1936

What a Nice Municipal Park, Harms, Inc., 1935

What Do You Think about Men?, Cole Porter, 1955

What Is That Tune?, Chappell & Co., Inc., 1938

What Is This Thing Called Love?, Harms, Inc., 1929

What Shall I Do?, Chappell & Co., Inc., 1938

What–Should–I–Do?, Chappell & Co., Inc., 1938

When I Had a Uniform On, T. B. Harms and Francis, Day and Hunter, 1919

When I Used to Lead the Ballet (Collaboration with T. Lawrason Riggs), G. Schirmer, 1916

When I Was a Little Cuckoo, Chappell & Co., Inc., 1945

When Love Beckoned, Chappell & Co., Inc., 1939

When Love Comes Your Way, Harms, Inc., 1933

When Me, Mowgli Love, Harms, Inc., 1935

When My Baby Goes to Town, Chappell & Co., Inc., 1943

When My Caravan Comes Home, Harms, Inc., 1922

Where Have You Been?, Harms, Inc., 1930

Where Is the Life That Late I Led?, Cole Porter, 1949

Where, Oh Where?, Cole Porter, 1949

Wherever They Fly the Flag of Ole England, Chappell & Co., Inc., 1946

Which?, Harms, Inc., 1928

Who Knows?, Chappell & Co., Inc., 1937

Who Said Gay Paree?, Cole Porter, 1952

Who Wants to Be a Millionaire?, Loew's, Inc., 1955

Who Would Have Dreamed?, Chappell & Co., Inc., 1940

Why Am I So Gone about That Gal?, Buxton Hill Music Corp., 1957

Why Can't You Behave?, Cole Porter, 1948

Why Didn't We Meet Before? (Words by Clifford Grey), Chappell & Co., Ltd., 1920

Why Do You Want to Hurt Me So?, Cole Porter, 1950

Why Should I Care?, Chappell & Co., Inc., 1937

Why Shouldn't I?, Harms, Inc., 1935

Without Love, Cole Porter, 1954

Wond'ring Night and Day, Chappell & Co., Ltd., 1922

Wouldn't It Be Fun!, Cole Porter, 1958

Wow-Ooh-Wolf, Chappell & Co., Inc., 1945

Wunderbar, Cole Porter, 1948

You and Me, Harms, Inc., 1928

You Can Do No Wrong, Chappell & Co., Inc., 1948

You Do Something to Me, Harms, Inc., 1929

You Don't Know Paree, Harms, Inc., 1929

You Don't Remind Me, Cole Porter, 1949

You Irritate Me So, Chappell & Co., Inc., 1941

You Never Know, Chappell & Co., Inc., 1938

You'd Be So Nice To Come Home To, Chappell & Co., Inc., 1942

You're a Bad Influence on Me, Chappell & Co., Inc., 1936

You're in Love, Harms, Inc., 1932

You're Just Too, Too, Loew's, Inc., 1956
You're Sensational, Buxton Hill Music Corp., 1955
You're the Top, Harms, Inc., 1934
You're Too Far Away, Harms, Inc., 1934
Yours, Harms, Inc., 1935
You've Got Something, Chappell & Co., Inc., 1936
You've Got That Thing, Harms, Inc., 1929